# Psychics, Crooks and unexplained phenomena

To the future!
May all the experiences
be positive and exciting!
Wolfgang
September 2005

# Psychics, Crooks and unexplained phenomena

*Wolfgang Schmidt*

Writers Club Press
San Jose New York Lincoln Shanghai

**Psychics, Crooks and unexplained phenomena**



Writers Club Press
an imprint of iUniverse, Inc.

For information address:
iUniverse, Inc.
5220 S. 16th St., Suite 200
Lincoln, NE 68512
www.iuniverse.com

ISBN: 0-595-25022-X

Printed in the United States of America

# *Contents*

# 1

# *Madame Rosita is a Crook!*

*My first experience with a psychic was a flop. It accounted for a lot of my skepticism in my further search—*

Madame Rosita was sitting in front of me and I could not help but think of her as a typical gypsy, the kind I had seen many times in paintings or in movies. The long black hair fell over her shoulders and while I could not see her ears, I was betting with myself that normally she would wear big looped earrings.

When I had phoned to make an appointment she had not asked me any questions other than my name, and now that I was sitting in her living room she was talking to another person on the phone. Her mother tongue seemed to be a Latin language, but I could not be sure, as I did not understand her words.

Looking at her, I noticed a long, bulky black dress with white and red patterns stitched into what I presumed was cotton. She also had a red scarf around her shoulders with a brooch holding the ends together on the right side of her chest.

I felt uncomfortable.

In the classified section of the newspaper there had been an advertisement under "personal" offering psychic readings with guaranteed accuracy. The phone number had indicated the west-end of the city and I made the appointment.

It was my first experience with a psychic and I did not know how to behave. "Stay cool", I said to myself.

Her phone conversation appeared to be nearing the end. Madame Rosita gestured to me to wait one more minute and she would be with me.

On the table between us lay a deck of cards, some papers, magazines and a Bible. 'A funny combination', I thought to myself.

I looked around the room. Other than a chesterfield with cushions in black velvet with gold embroidery, two side tables, a coffee table and a dining room cabinet full of miniatures, there was only the coffee table with 4 chairs. One occupied by a black and white cat, one empty, and the two we were sitting on.

"O.K.", said Madame Rosita, looking at me and hanging up the phone. "Sorry for the waiting."

She spoke English with a heavy accent. Portuguese or Hungarian came to my mind.

"Would you like me to use cards"?

I told her that I would prefer she use psychic powers, as advertised in the paper.

"O.K.", she said.

She stared at me for a while, then closed her eyes and murmured something I could not understand. I leaned forward to listen but then she spoke with her natural voice and said: "There are a lot of black clouds around you".

Her arms made a moving gesture to emphasize a lot of air around my body. "Lots of black", she repeated.

I had read about psychics going into a trance and having to be undisturbed during the session but Madame Rosita did not seem to be in a trance, and I asked, "What do the black clouds mean"?

"Trrouble", she answered, closing her eyes again. "Lots of trrouble". She rolled the 'r' like a musical note.

"Your family has lots of trrouble too, your wife is pushed by an evil force and that brings lots of trrouble for your family".

Admittedly, goose pimples appeared on my skin.

What followed was a barrage of claims about my family and how I was suffering from evil influences. It sounded as though my relationships with my mother and my wife were particularly bad, and children were suffering because I did not realize all the black clouds (cum evil influences) were around me.

Madame Rosita spoke in such an assertive manner that I could hardly interrupt to tell her that my mother had passed on many years ago and that there was no wife and there were no children suffering.

She was rolling the words in one long stream, ending up with the hope that I would soon be better off financially, because she could see that presently my money situation was not very good.

But, there was a light at the end of the tunnel of my suffering: It would take a lot of work and I would meet a good friend to help me to get over my sufferings and my family's suffering. "A lot of prayers are needed…"

At this point Madame Rosita grabbed the Bible and handed it to me and almost yelled, "Quickly say a prayer. The evil forces are coming in right now and we need protection".

I took the Bible, closed my eyes and actually said a short prayer. I asked for forgiveness (for my attitude) because, in my opinion, the statements made by Madame Psychic were nothing but horsefeathers.

"That's seven dollars", said Rosita in a whisper. Her body leaned over the table towards me and she appeared very concerned. "I have to talk to you privately afterwards".

I don't know who she thought was listening, because I did not see anybody overhearing our conversation. She gestured for me to give her the money. I did, and miraculously, the money disappeared into a fold of her black dress.

She took my hand and led me toward the chesterfield, sort of looking over her shoulder, as if there were others at the table. I looked. The cat was still sleeping and no other beings were in sight.

In a hushed voice Madame Rosita whispered, “You must listen to me, the evil forces around you will harm you. I can help you”.

Wondering what this was all about and feeling that maybe now was the time to dash to the door, I stood silent. She must have taken that as the symbol of agreement because she said “Right. You have to protect yourself and I can help you. Let me light a candle and let’s sit down to talk.”

It sure was not my idea of an idyllic tête-à-tête by candlelight. And obviously this was not what she had in her mind either.

Sitting next to me on the chesterfield with a lit candle on the side table Madame Rosita whispered to me “There are many evil forces, too many for you alone to handle. I will be your friend. I will light a candle every day for you and I will pray with you and for you, every day three times to protect you. No?”

Even though she said no, it was a gesture of agreement for me to say yes. I shook my head and said, “Well, I don’t know what’s involved”.

And then I got it—with both barrels.

“Give me one hundred dollars and I will be your friend and take the spell of evil forces off you and your family. You will all be happy and you will make lots and lots of money. You will sleep deep and I will make you happy without evil forces.”

Madame Rosita said this in an urgent way, as though the evil forces were already sitting on my shoulder to take my soul…and maybe my body.

I told her that she had been right all along and that I had a lot of financial problems and that I did not have a hundred dollars—evil or no evil.

Little did I know that the Psychic was not so easily dissuaded. She gave me ideas as to how to get the money; from going to the bank or the pawnshop to soliciting all my friends.

The more I was unwilling to follow her suggestions the more urgent her voice became, and louder by the minute. I stood up, preparing to leave the house. I walked towards the door. Behind me a tirade of worrisome threats telling me that I was not familiar with spirit power. Warning me that I did not know how to overcome evil threats and I did not appreciate her being my friend. After all, she was offering to do all this for a mere hundred where others would charge thousands.

As I was turning the doorknob, she grabbed my arm.

"To show you how much of a friend I am willing to be, I will do the work for free. I will pray for you and I will remove the evil from you—no cost. O.K.?"

I really did not want her to pray for me and I wasn't sure that I needed it. But with her offer of free praying—well, what did I have to lose.

"O.K.", I said, "if you want to pray for me free of charge, by all means, you go ahead".

My hand turned the knob and I opened the door wide to let myself out.

"Good" she said, "I will pray to make you lots of money. Give me fifty dollars to pay for the candles".

I quickly slipped out. Her outstretched arm did not catch me, and the barrage of words, some of them in the foreign language, hardly reached my ear.

My car was parked around the block. Sitting inside I took a deep breath of relief.

I looked at myself in the rear-view mirror. Was I shaking? Was I worried about the evil forces? An unshaven face looked back at me, not worried. It could belong to someone with problems, "lots of family problems"—but it didn't.

Looking down at my attire I could see how the lady was getting some of her information. My jeans were faded, well worn. My Cowboy boots showed a lot of wear and tear. No jewellery on my hands. She must have thought she was talking to an unemployed factory worker—truck driver maybe?

I turned the key in my sports Audi and left the West End behind me.

# 2

## *Is there such a thing as a past life?*

◆

***I thought that a regression might reveal some truth. For me it did not, personally. But it gave me something to think about—***

The promise was to get you back into a former lifetime. Well, after reading the advertisement, I immediately phoned for a reservation.

"Bring a pillow and a pen"—those were the instructions, besides getting the amount I would have to pay in cash at the door. The name of the hotel and the room were given as well.

The Lady was advertised as a professor from the west coast, doing research into past lives. Apparently, she had worked out a system which could get you back into a previous life and return you to the present—with you remembering facts and figures from the past.

When the time arrived, I could not wait to get to the ballroom of the hotel where the whole procedure was taking place. I thought I was early, but the room was already crowded. People, young, old and in between were laying on the floor, with their head on pillows. Music was playing and there was no conversation.

The usher, after taking my money, pointed to a spot for me to take. It was near the window and quite far from the area where a microphone and a lectern had been set up. I told the young woman that I was doing research myself and would appreciate a place a bit up-front. She was obliging and I ended up in the front row on the outside. This suited me fine, as I could look around without disturbing anyone.

When I passed on my money, I was handed a bunch of papers, which turned out to be questionnaires.

I don't think the fire marshal would have approved of the number of participants laying on the floor, but that was not my concern. It surprised me, though, how many people wanted to take a trip back down memory lane. My guess was about 500.

The music stopped and a lady in her 60's walked in. She had a certain air of confidence around her which made the place hush. One could have heard a needle drop.

"Ok, sit up and listen. You know my name, you know my work. Let's get right to it. I will hypnotize you and you will follow my instructions to go back to a former life time. You will remember what you have done and who you were then and you will come back and report to me.

"You all have received a number of questionnaires. They are to be completed after each trip. Let's get to it and not waste any time. If you have any doubts just sit there and keep quiet. If you feel afraid, now is the time to leave. Once we start, I don't want any interruptions. Is anyone in here who is under doctors care and has taken medication?"

There were a few hands and she questioned the people. It did not seem to matter what their problem was, because they were allowed to stay and participate.

The music came back, but just very softly as background. Our professor started to go into a relaxation exercise with the group. From there, we went into group hypnosis.

To my regret, I must admit that when I woke up next, I was coming back from a deep sleep. I was sure that I had been snoring away, not noticing anything—not remembering anything. The last words I heard before falling asleep were "going deeper into hypnosis".

I looked at the paper with the questions and could not answer any. There was no place, no time, no name to recall.

To my amazement, the people around me were busy filling in the blanks. Just the odd person seemed to be like me, without an experience.

My plan was laid: After all the questionnaires were collected, the next session started. As the professor counted down the hypnosis path, I started humming in my own mind, all to myself. I did not want to listen to her voice. I did not want to go into hypnosis. I wanted to see what was going on around me.

Finally the deep trance was announced and while I kept my eyes closed I sort of squinted around to see the action.

Nothing happened. The group got instructions to go back in time; to observe and report. Now I opened my eyes and looked around. The faces of the people nearby were easily recognizable and I noticed on some of them an expression of bliss. Others seemed to worry and others again were just blank.

A woman in the middle of the group started to wince and whine. The professor went over and placed her hand on the woman's shoulder, reassuring her that she was in hypnosis and that the experiences she felt were long past. She would be only an observer now and feel no pain, emotion etc. It seemed to help.

She asked the same questions which were on the questionnaire and everyone got the command to "remember".

The group really had to dig. They were asked to look at their clothes, their money, their homes. Friends and relatives were accounted for, as was the date or time period in which they had landed. Leading political figures and customs of the day were to be remembered. All in all, their answers would give a well rounded picture of the former life—if it existed.

Wake-up time came and almost everyone was filling out the questionnaire again. The faces showed smiles, some had grim expressions, but in general eager to write. Some must have been either nowhere or asleep like I was before. They just looked around and had nothing to write. Just guessing, I would say that over 90% of the people present were writing—and writing fast.

I tried to peak at the sheet of my neighbor, but my clumsy attempt was swatted with an indignant look from the writer.

Papers collected, the third session started.

Now I wanted to be part of it again. I was eager to follow the instructions to relax and to "go down into hypnosis".

"By one, you will be wide awake and report". I woke up—nothing had happened.

It seemed that I had been sleeping again. I stared at the questionnaire—nothing came to me. No memories of a trip, no memories of a past life.

Maybe I've never lived before? Yeah, that could be the answer. No past, just a present. I really tried to believe it, but when I saw again all those people writing quickly into the blank spaces, I wondered.

Five sessions in all and not one was successful for me. When question and answer period came, I was right there.

'Why was I falling asleep'? 'Why could I not remember anything'? Her answer was not satisfactory to me. "Needing to keep my past lives secret from the present life"—well, how about the others?

More questions were asked and the professor was very short in answers. The research was not completed yet. All was only a theory. We were part of the research—maybe one day we would all know. In the meantime, watch for the results in an upcoming book.

What a sales pitch.

I started to believe that the people who so eagerly wrote to fill in the blanks were just imagining things. They had probably slept, too, but had a good dream. Maybe they had some desires to be Cleopatra or Caesar or Romeo or an Apache Warrior and in their hypnosis just acted out what they had read or dreamed about.

A group of participants drifted to the hotel cafeteria. I just listened as they discussed their experiences. Wow, a movie could not have been better.

One young lady apparently had woke up in Scotland. She was a peasant girl and her father was away in some war. Her mother and her sister had to work the fields. No money, no time, but ample dress description, neighbors names and a Queen's name. She remembered a little church and described a church ceremony—quite different from today.

Maybe she had read some books about church services in earlier days.

A man in his sixties seemed to have landed in the Middle East. He told of his nomadic life style and of a few details, which a skeptic like myself could have attributed to books and tourism.

All in all, I was not that much impressed, but then I did not have enough information to make a judgment. Most of the people in the cafeteria had had an experience and were satisfied that they had experienced a previous lifetime.

Maybe I was just jealous.

## ***years later***

I had occasion to travel to the west coast and wanted to visit the professor. She had finished her research and had published the results which were overwhelmingly in favor of the existence of past lives.

Unfortunately, she was on a lecture tour and I was out of luck.

I did speak to an assistant on the project and would like to relay one story, as told second hand, without checking the facts. Fascinating nevertheless and with names and dates which I could check if I wanted to:

One of the many persons researched in individual sessions came to view one of her past lives in the Middle East. This was early in the professor's career and apparently she too just wanted to find proof, either way.

The clients name was Kathy and she was an easy hypnotic subject. Once in trance she spoke of the market place in her little village where she was buying spices and nuts.

She had coins in her hand and she remembered the pictures on both sides. After she woke up she was able to draw a coin in detail.

The professor went to the local museum where a colleague of hers was very familiar with historical finds in the Middle East. He looked at the drawing and shook his head.

"The picture doesn't make sense", he commented. "No coin like that has ever been found, nor is it known to historians or archeologists", was his conclusion after about three weeks of searching in his circle of expert colleagues.

Four months after the hypnosis session with Kathy, which produced the drawing of the coin, the professor received a call from her museum colleague. He wanted her to drop by the house as quickly as she could.

There was no indication as to what the call was all about, and she visited him three days later. After all the preliminary talk, the colleague showed her a magazine and pointed to an article on a recent dig in Turkey.

A pottery vase was illustrated in glorious four colors as a double spread in the magazine. The vase had retained the fine engravings and the color decoration appeared as though it was done yesterday.

The professor looked at the vase and shrugged. "What about it?", she wanted to know. Her colleague was excited and she could not understand his anxious behavior.

"Don't you see?", he almost shouted.

"See what, the decoration?" she asked.

"No, no, no. The coin, the coin!"

With growing excitement he pointed at the side of the vase, where a few coins and tools had been placed. All had come from the same dig.

She almost fainted. There it was: the head on the coin, the inscription and the shape—all identical to Kathy's drawing.

"I have made some calls already and would you believe that the archeological team found these items the same day as your student drew the picture!"

He spoke fast and much louder than necessary.

"Even the time could be almost to the minute the same, taking the time difference into consideration."

He sat down, shaking his head.

As I listened to the story, a shiver went along my spine. Could this be coincidence?

The assistant did not think so…and apparently neither did the professor.

# 3

# *Do the stars predict your future?*

✦

## *Doing a good deed (a leftover habit from my Boy Scout days) earned me a horoscope. What a revelation—*

Three little old ladies stood in front of the church. The cold November winds made them huddle together for protection. They wanted to take the bus home and still had about fifteen minutes to wait.

It was Saturday night and I had nothing better planned—I offered them a ride home in my car. They were surprised, talked and accepted.

All three lived quite far apart in the city. I delivered them in front of their respective houses and apartment buildings.

Just when the last lady was ready to leave my car she asked me, "When were you born?" I told her. "Ahhh," she said "I thought that much, a Saggy".

I did not know what she was up to, but she was obviously referring to the astrological sign I was born under: Sagittarius.

She asked me a few more questions, like exactly what time I was born, the town and country of my birth, and she asked me for my phone number. I handed her my business card as she went into the apartment building. I could see her standing in front of the elevators and I waited until she stepped into one.

I turned my car around and left. "Silly me," I thought," I never asked the lady for her name.

My ride home was uneventful. I had had a hectic day and was glad to go to sleep.

I woke up on Sunday morning, about seven, my usual time. For a moment I considered whether to linger and read, but then decided to go for breakfast.

Around eight thirty I had the urge to go to the office. I felt that some work had been left undone and that I should look it over.

While I do not work Sundays, I do however believe that if something has to be done, it has to be done, regardless of the time or the day. I made my way downtown.

The moment I entered the reception area the phone started to ring. I went to the switchboard to answer. "Probably a wrong number", I thought while fiddling with the buttons to get the call.

Without formalities or hello, the voice on the other end said, "I knew you would be in the office at nine. I worked all night and finished at six this morning. When I wanted to phone you I noticed that your business card showed only your office number....".

It was the lady I had delivered to the apartment last night. I told her that today was Sunday and that it was highly unusual for me to be in the office or even answer the telephone on Sunday. She should consider herself lucky that she had reached me.

She brushed my remarks aside. "That's what you think. I need to see you to give you something. Can you come over here right now?"

I was more than surprised.

The night before, the ladies had given me directions as I drove and I had not paid attention to exactly where I had dropped them off, so I needed her address again. Remembering that it was an apartment building, I asked for the suite number. "Never mind", she said, "I will meet you downstairs in the hall".

What could I say? I left immediately.

While driving to her address, I thought, "I haven't even looked at my desk to see why I felt I had to come into the office in the first place".

The sun was shining now and it had become one of those crisp autumn days when one can feel that winter is not far away; bright sky and sunshine.

The streets were clear, no traffic, no pedestrians, a little too early for the Sunday morning church crowd. I made it to the apartment building in record time.

Stepping into the lobby, the elevator door opened and the lady stepped out. She was wearing a housecoat and looked cheerful; not at all like someone who had napped for only three hours. She handed me an envelope.

"There will be more in about three months". With that she turned around and stepped back into the elevator. The doors closed, and as I came out of my daze I was standing alone in the lobby, holding a brown envelope with my name and birthday written on it.

I ambled to my car, still perplexed, thinking about the lady: No explanation, no greeting, nothing...just the envelope.

I became curious.

The first restaurant enroute was a Pancake House. Not too busy; the waitress had obviously expected to serve me a full breakfast but I told her that a coffee would do.

The white paper sheets in the envelope where handwritten. "Old fashioned" came into my mind.

First there was a letter. In it she told me that she had looked at my birth constellations and that she had gotten excited about my life. She had found more and more information and had written it down. Before she realized it, it was early morning. Because of the many exciting things that were going to happen to me she wanted to inform me immediately.

Grabbing my business card she realized that my home phone number was not on it. She meditated briefly and went to sleep. "The rest you know", she wrote. "I will send you some more information soon."

The remaining sheets, I realized were my horoscope.

I had never had a horoscope done for me. Sure I sometimes looked in the newspaper at the humorous directions for the day, but I did not believe in them anymore than I believe in Santa Claus. Some positive thinking—a bit of life's wisdom—a good income for the writer.

I started to read. At first a bunch of numbers and drawings, notes about the sun, the moon and the stars. Some astrological gobbledygook like trines, transits, rising sign.... I just scanned without reading until the distinct handwriting held my eye ".... highly intuitive, poetic, and sensitive position with an adaptability that makes it possible for you to use your abilities in almost any field that you want to."

The coffee was served and I covered the papers. I did not want the waitress to think of me as a kook.

"Whether you select a business, professional or artistic career, you are likely to master and understand it."

My back straightened as I sipped my coffee. Maybe the lady was right in her description.

"You are capable of broad abstractions of thought—of understanding details of philosophy...."

My coffee was cold when I picked up the cup next. I was so engrossed in reading the pages that I had forgotten my surroundings.

I got up, paid and went straight home.

Leafing again through the pages I was amazed how accurately the lady described my character. "...you get too easily interested in the new. Seek in all things depth and quality, rather than quantity; in love, concentration rather than variety".

Predictions for the future followed, and I must say that from this day on I had second thoughts about Astrology.

About three months later a brown envelope arrived in my office. No return address, no name. I opened it and knew immediately from the distinct handwriting that my "little old lady" had kept her word and sent me more information.

It was too busy in the office to read that stuff, so I tucked it into my briefcase and planned to take it home.

At lunch time my curiosity got the better of me and I grabbed the envelope, munched a sandwich and read: "Contemplating again the eye catching hallmarks of your chart, I wonder what I wrote so far a few months ago. Hopefully, I will not repeat anything, although it is worth pointing out again, that your..." Now came some symbols and a note: "Please follow your chart now while reading..." and again "...read chart......"

She told me that I was a very freedom-loving person; attached, yes, but with no strings.

"People respect you for getting things done without 'fanfare' but with splendid results...".

The lady sure knew how to boost my ego and of course I agreed with her on all the strong and good attributes of my character. I forget now, whether there were any negative things in her Letter. I probably just skipped over them and forgot them as quickly as possible. After all, I am a positive thinker. No use dwelling on character faults.

She must have spent hours and hours, probably days, on the horoscope and I wanted to thank her and see whether I could do something for her.

I drove to the apartment building and, standing in the lobby, I realized that I did not know her name; did not know her phone number or even the apartment number. After hanging around the building for half an hour, giving some tenants walking in and out a description of her, I decided that it was useless and went home.

Sometime later, I drove by the church building again, where I had picked up the three ladies. Maybe she would be there—but it was not to be. I sent her a quiet "thank you" through the air waves.

Many of the predictions in my horoscope came true. Was it because I expected them? Was it because the stars can predict?

# 4

# *Visiting the Crystal Skull with a psychologist, who made me laugh, and with a blind man who could see.*

*Crystals are thought of as transmitters of unseen power, and the Crystal Skull is thought to represent an earlier civilization. I did not find the power of the Skull—but a powerful postcard—*

I was introduced to him without knowing why he was in town. He was blind, walked with a white cane and had his girlfriend lead him by the arm most of the time.

California was his home and he had a shop along the main coastal highway where he sold crystals. According to a mutual friend he knew everything there was to know about crystals.

We are not talking about crystals for computers or watches, we are talking about the real thing. The stuff that mother nature produces which looks like spikes made out of glass.

Mind you, I did not know then and can hardly comprehend now that crystals in computers are tiny slivers of the real thing.

I also did not know that the Silicon Valley in California was not a real place name but just a generic description of an industrial area chock full of computer geeks. And Silicon as a nonmetallic element is of great importance to man and constitutes over 25% of the earth's crust—only the second most abundant element on earth, after oxygen.

My blind acquaintance talked about the healing qualities and the vibratory rate of crystals. He explained to me that the crystal stores information which you can read, if you know how to do it.

I was about to see a demonstration of a reading. My friend had arranged to go to a place nearby where a lady owned a crystal skull.

Many years ago I had read in a magazine about this strange skull, which had apparently come from a by-gone era—a civilization that had once lived in South America and had been very much advanced compared with our technology today.

Some experts say that the skull is void of tool marks and that the shape, the features and holes for the eyes could not be reproduced even with today's technology.

A roaming archaeologist is credited with finding the skull in South America—but somehow, the story changes with time.

Nevertheless, the current owner is the spinster daughter of the archaeologist. She was either with her father when it was discovered, or she found it herself and showed her father....

About 20 people had gathered in the living room of the skull owner, who lived in a house with a lady companion and two beautiful dogs—and the skull of course. One of the guests was the blind crystal expert, another was a famous psychologist who has written several books on the paranormal. Also, as a great fan of Nicola Teslar, he dabbled in technology. Radio waves and electro-magnetic beams were his specialty. He was ready to 'read' the skull right after the Californian gave it a try.

The group entered into silence, everyone concentrated on the skull after touching it. On the table, reflecting the lights from the window, sat the skull; in front of it the blind man, oblivious to the group—meditating.

After a while he started to mumble. At first a few words, then the sentences became more coherent. He talked about a great spiritual leader in our midst; talked about a scene from a long ago past, mentioned the age of the skull, (I forgot the years), and forecast that the skull needed a permanent home and that someone in the audience would find it one.

Members of the group were in deep meditation. Only their breathing could be heard. All eyes were closed. Only mine were opened from time to time to take in the reaction of the people around me.

The messages of the blind man did not turn me on. Things he said were common knowledge and other predictions were either flattery to a person in the room or something too weird to remember.

Then the psychologist was prompted to continue the reading. He apparently was the great master communicator. Some greater, wiser power had elected to give us the true knowledge—the wisdom of the ages, according to the blind man.

The psychologist, (he was fully qualified, also had an MD and lectured and wrote on parapsychology and psychic research) moved closer to the skull. He took off his wristwatch and laid it over his head. With his hands on the skull and his eyes closed, he started to talk.

He mentioned that his messages came from the commander of the seventh space orbiter (or something like that) who needed to tell the world about the forthcoming new age with the enlightenment to follow. All of us would be engulfed in love and the aliens would be among us. Friendly, peaceful, highly civilized, "these aliens are coming in peace" and want us to be prepared.

The skull was going to be a communication vehicle. It needed a permanent home to be accessible to many people and to be touched by many, as it had been in the early days when it was used for healing purposes.

I just had to keep on looking at the psychologist's head. The watch laying over the scalp with the thinning hair—it looked too funny. I had to control myself not to burst out laughing. How could an educated man like he come up with all this nonsense.

His pilot's watch sure looked more than ridiculous on his head and the story about the aliens did not sound any more credible by his acting in this strange manner.

A combined prayer ended the meeting. Coffee, tea and cookies were available.

I ambled towards the psychologist. He talked to the spinster and really impressed her. When the time came to put a question to him I expressed curiosity about his watch, why it was on his head during his reading of the skull. The Doctor said simply "the commander told me to do so."

Well, I often heard about psychologists and psychiatrists losing touch with reality because they were dealing too much with their patients' imagination. But this was just too much. He needed to explain more.

To make a long story short, he claimed to have some UFO experiences whereby he had been given instruction to do certain things.

He was guided to act as he acted.

Controlling the facial expressions and looking serious when you want to scream out laughing is not easy. I thought I did pretty well in this conversation. This man was intelligent. I could not make up my mind whether he took all the people for a ride or whether he really believed his own story.

The blind man and his girlfriend were munching on the cookies. He talked to a lady who was into crystal healing and gave her advice about the shape, color and clarity of the stones. I asked him about his background, what his education was and how he learned about the healing power, etc.

Unfortunately nothing of any sense was said. His education was minimal, his learning gleaned from books and his "real knowledge" came through psychic impressions.

I wanted to know how he lost his sight and why the crystals wouldn't help him in restoring his eyesight.

His answer was simple; that he did not want to talk about it. I politely excused myself and wandered to the next group.

The afternoon went by quickly. Arrangements were made to have dinner in a restaurant. A number of people got together and the blind man, his girlfriend, the psychologist and two others decided to join. I was part of the group.

At the restaurant I sat opposite the blind man and next to the psychologist.

While talking to the latter, I closely watched the blind man because I wanted to know how he would handle his food. To my surprise he managed knife and fork very well, selected food to eat and some to leave on the plate.

I became very suspicious.

After coffee, we went to our cars.

Making it appear like an accident, I came very close to the white cane of the blind man who seemed to search his way through the parking lot, listening to the shouted direction from his girlfriend who had already unlocked their car.

The cane did not touch me and the blind man stopped in front of me. He could not possibly know that I was standing in front of him.

"You must be able to see something", I said to him. "The way you handled your food and the way you noticed me as an obstacle in the way, you must be able to see".

He did not answer at first.

When I pushed "Well, can you see?", he answered "No, I chose not to see". With that, he walked to the car without using his cane.

While we were in the house, he and I had exchanged business cards, because I was planning on going to California on a business trip. Stopping by his crystal shop on my way would have been my plan.

Needless to say I discarded the idea to see his shop—after the episode in the parking lot.

I told the psychologist about my conversation with the blind man and he just said "he is looking inward now, because the outer world upsets him too much. He is learning from the inside out, he is a great psychic".

One can imagine that I had my doubts about a fake blind guy who had not given any indication about his psychic ability.

It was many years later when one day I received a post card from California. The photo showed beautiful mountain scenery. The writing part was filled with only a few words in a shaky but decipherable script: "The time will come when all the blind will see. Your father says that he has joined his spouse. Rejoice. Love. Your 'blind' friend Bob".

I was shocked. Immediately I knew who the writer was. My family affairs were never discussed with him and the date of the postage stamp was two days *before* my father's passing to the other side of life. I had just returned from his funeral in Europe. My Mother had passed over some 25 years ago.

Yes, I was shocked.

# 5

## *There is information in books.*

◆

***I read and read and read. And the more I read, the more I needed to know. This reading list is only a drop in the ocean of wisdom. But is it meaningful?—***

I was intrigued by the power displayed by the various psychics. It appeared to me that knowing someone on the other side could be good for business. How would one go about finding the ghost, spirit, guide or whatever they called it? Obviously, I had to find some books to get some answers.

In the early 50's it appeared that those who wrote about of psychic phenomena had to go underground to get information published. The type of books I began finding from that era were published privately. Much of the information came in pamphlet form, some in duplicated typewritten sheets.

I was well on my way to exploring a new world, a world with new dimensions, or, as spiritualists called it "a house with many mansions". (This is a quote from the New Testament of the Bible, often used to link Jesus Christ with the present practices of spiritualism (John 14:2).)

Traveling through Great Britain, I found many spiritualist 'churches', usually small congregations with services which included "messages from the other side of life". The groups were often located in basements, storefronts or in people's homes. There were pamphlets and books available for the student of spiritualism. The church organizations had manuals for sale which included "spiritual and psychic development".

In some obscure magazines, I noticed small advertisements for information on secret societies. After applying for membership one would be inducted into the art of reading other people's minds or to communicate with bodiless entities. There seemed to be a regular underground business going on, teaching this sort of thing.

Mystic schools had been around for centuries. They were in ancient Greece, in Egypt; they flourished throughout the Roman Empire; and according to some, Jesus of Nazareth belonged to one of the secret societies and taught the ancient wisdom as a master teacher.

Once the Christian Church was in power and dominated the then western world, many of those groups, the Gnostics, were wiped out. Heretics to the church dogma were burned at the stake.

Whatever was left got into the clutches of Adolf Hitler who managed to burn some books and unify Free Masons, Rosicrucians, Jews and Catholic priests...in concentration camps.

It is surprising that some of the knowledge taught by those mystic societies still exists in print today. In North America at least two large organizations fight for the "right" to be the legitimate successor of the "true Rosicrucian order". Whatever the real truth about that one may be, their publications are a gold mine for the student of the occult.

One of the organizations works on membership and secret dispensation of knowledge. Small pamphlets are mailed once a month and the member has to vow not to reveal the knowledge or the teaching material to any other person. The student learns to use his or her mind to contact other members through "Astro travel", even if it is not called exactly that. It will take years to develop that skill but the promise is there.

The other group of the same persuasion publishes their literature freely and at reasonable prices. Here one can learn about the creation of the world, the previous seen and unseen worlds, Atlantis and the secret brotherhood of the society.

There is one common thread throughout the teaching of the various mystic schools, from Masons to religious orders: God is around us, in us and we are part of the total creation and creators. There is a power within us which we do not recognize or practice. We have responsibilities to our environment and our fellow man. Soon, there will be a great change in our world structure...and we better prepare ourselves.

All of them teach their students to be of good character and a contributor to society.

Also in the 50's a few books appeared in North America, which had mystical overtones, not that is was right away recognizable: U.S. Anderson wrote "Three Magic Words"—it became a bestseller.

It was renamed from "The Key to Power and Personal Peace". The message was simple: "If thou canst but believe—All things are possible to him who believes".

Anderson was popular and wrote "The Secret of Secrets" only a few years later. Here he reveals "...how the spiritual realization of an indwelling God may be applied to the various problems of everyday living."

Attitude, thinking, mind control...there is a thread going through all the books linking our conscious mind to the eternal creative force. But then, is this anything new?

Hebrew tradition demands faith. Eastern religions teach the overcoming of the body to have the union with the creator...in modern thinking mind over matter.

"Therefore I tell you, do not be anxious about your life, what you shall eat, nor about your body, what you shall put on. For life is more than food, and the body more than clothing." Luke 12:22.

And to get in touch with the Archetypes of the collective unconscious was one of Carl Gustav Jung's contribution to psychology.

Religion in that respect could also be part of pathology according to Jung's "Psychology and Religion", which he wrote in 1938.

Psychology and Psychiatry did investigate the super natural mind, only to find in most cases an abnormal behavior. A good overview is given in the book Psychiatry and Mysticism, edited by Stanley R. Dean (1975).

The mystic schools had different opinions about the subject, as Elbert Benjamine wrote for the Church of Light in 1936 in a book "Doctrine of Esoteric Psychology". He worked not only on the basis of astrology, but had a lot to say about the power of suggestion; how to develop creative imagination; how to cultivate subliminal thinking and how to use affirmation.

While Benjamine was read mostly within the occult schools, a contemporary of his hit the masses with "Think and Grow Rich".

Napoleon Hill wrote the blue print for a successful life. Amazingly he also suggested to work with "infinite intelligence", the sixth sense and the power of imagination. He reported that some of the figures he had imagined became real and gave real information. Spirits? Guides? Witchcraft?

Hill is still very popular. His books are still bestsellers today, as they were over 50 years ago.

The positive attitude prescription of Hill is also demanded by Norman Vincent Peale who is known as the father of the "Power of Positive Thinking". Peale says in his book "You can if you think you can" that we all have personal powers within ourselves that can lead to a solution of our daily problems.

Neither Hill nor Peale tell us how to become psychic in so many words, but the message is clear: go within and you get answers "seemingly out of nowhere".

Emanuel Swedenborg was a scientist, diplomat and philosopher. His works are still in bookstores around the world and a "New Church" is following his teachings. He had some psychic experiences which convinced him that there was more to life than our mind could comprehend.

Researchers, clergy, politicians and others tried to discredit many of the persons who would come forward and tell the world of their unusual experiences. However many well documented cases have survived. Swedenborg is described in "The Presence of other Worlds" by Wilson Van Dusen.

A good account of the workings of a psychic is given by Charles Hapgood in "Voices of Spirit". Here the messages of psychic Elwood Babbitt are documented.

Some Christian preachers still call psychic phenomenon the work of the devil. It is compared with witchcraft, fortune telling and necromancy. Quotes from the Bible are used to substantiate their claim. Because of the fierce attacks on spiritual churches and psychics, scientists were not very eager to wage war on the side of the unknown.

In recent years however, best-selling paperbacks about the subject and a greater interest in the general public made some scholars daring enough to put their name in print dealing with occult subject matters.

Sheila Ostrander and Lynn Schroeder told us in "Psychic Discoveries Behind the Iron Curtain" of research in official laboratories from Prague to Moscow. Suddenly America was listening. Could it be possible that physical objects could be moved by mind power?

For many years a lone voice in the wilderness had studied Extra Sensory Perception (ESP). Dr. J. B. Rhine conducted thousands of tests in Durham, North Carolina. He is considered the dean of American parapsychology. The trials and tribulations he went through to establish scientific evidence for ESP and the debunking from fellow scientists is typical of the subject matter.

The mind seems to be the connecting point to the other worlds. It appears that one has to control the mind to make contact with the universal force. John Williams in "Wisdom of your subconscious mind" and Robert Ferguson in "Universal Mind" seem to link the cosmic forces to our well being, to our eternal search for God and to our happy and prosperous life here on earth.

The "Power of Mind" was well illustrated by Adam Smith. He examined diverse philosophies from Zen to EST, from Biofeedback to Yoga. Every mind trip of the 60's and 70's was taken into account.

Participating in the new awareness of mind power and capturing a market share in the new age literature, Carl Sagan wrote "Broca's Brain". In easy to understand language, Sagan presents the problems of Science and examines many of the messengers of the new age.

Following in the line-up of the revelations about Brain power comes Richard M. Restak, M.D. with "The Brain—the last frontier".

All of the publications hitting the occult section of the book stores created an awareness and a hunger for more information. History was presented by Eric Maple in "Witchcraft" and explicit directions on how to participate in the secret science of self-initiation is given by Francis King & Stephen Skinner in "Techniques of High Magic".

The passion for the occult in the nineteenth and twentieth century was examined by Ruth Brandon. She is asking in "The Spiritualists" what is was that attracted men such as William James, Conan Doyle and W. T. Stead to spiritualism?

A republished book from the 50's, "Witchcraft Today" by Gerald B. Gardner, reveals the secrets of the Witch cult.

Astro travel, out of body experiences, life after life accounts are documented by Brad Steiger in "Minds through Space and Time".

Is it a new phenomenon? Is it a passing fancy?

Not at all. It has been a concern of mankind probably from the beginning of man's consciousness. In 1913 the book "Mysticism in English literature" by Caroline Spurgeon, looks at poets and prose writers and examines love and nature stories throughout the ages to prove man's concern and quest.

Plato, Plotinus, Eckhart, Spinoza, Goethe and Hegel are quoted as falling into the category of Mystics.

What is Mysticism?

Spurgeon gives us a good explanation in her introduction by quoting the Concise Oxford Dictionary (1911) defining a mystic as "one who believes in spiritual apprehension of truths beyond the understanding".

That brings us back to the Rosicrucian's which claim to transmit the wisdom to make us understand. Max Heindel wrote in 1909 "The Rosicrucian Cosmo-Conception" which is the "Bible" of the followers of his group's philosophy. It will answer many questions about the earth and the universe—if you believe.

Another group adheres to the knowledge presented by H. Spencer Lewis who wrote in 1929 "Rosicrucian Principles for Home and Business". This book promises to "contain practical principles for the use of Cosmic Laws in the securing of better positions in life, the raising of money, the paying off of debts, the maintenance of health, the prevention of disease, and for bringing our ambitions into fulfillment and happy realization".

Last but not least another look behind the 'Iron Curtain'. In 1931 the Book "A new model of the Universe" was written by P. D. Ouspensky.

He analyzed schools of thought from the West and the East and connected them with modern ideas and explains them in the light of discoveries in his time. A sentence on the book cover reads: "Ouspensky clearly shows how ordinary knowledge is not of sufficient substance to bring about the transformation into a new man, for knowledge is not knowledge unless the part is related to the whole."

As we are at the beginning of a new century, we can expect more books to come—and go. Websites will glow with predictions and phenomena real or imagined. Many will be concerned with the prophecies of the past: the prediction of the end of the world. There will be many who advocate to move to "safe" areas; many who will ask to meet our Savior. Some may mean the spiritual Christ returning to Earth, some will set themselves up to be the Christ and others still will point to the heavens and the UFO's to look for last minute rescue.

The Mayan calendar ends in 2012 or 13, the 12th Planet is supposed to come close to Earth again, climate changes and pole shifting will threaten civilization. Zecharia Sitchin has written a whole raft of books called the 'Earth Chronicles', giving his interpretation of the Sumerian Clay Tablets the slant of an offshore civilization—the one that created us.

Oh, I should not forget, governments too have gotten into the psychic act not only behind the Iron Curtain, when it still existed. According to the "Psychic Warior" by David Morehouse the CIA had many study programmes in the works. Using 'remote viewers' they tried to spy behind the lines with out-of-body experiences or psychic impressions. Captain Morehouse exposed the various institutions involved in psychic research and apparently the work stopped.

Today, these 'psychic wariors' hire themselves out to private enterprise to help them. Some might call that psychic industrial espionage.

There will be books to teach quiet meditation, contemplation, prayer......

However, reading alone will not suffice. Practice is needed—if you believe that there is something there—to capture the unusual powers of the psychic world.

...and the search goes on.

# 6

# *Finding the psychics in a Church.*

## *Visiting a Spiritualist Church gives me a psychic impression and leaves me with a book list*

The Weekend paper carries a lot of church advertising and it is like the who's who in religion when one looks at the announced speakers, healers and mediums, yes mediums.

Having studied in the more traditional fields of philosophy, I was of course fully familiar with the mainline church organizations. But there were others, born from discontent of some members or by the vision of one person.

New ones sprang up all the time and some hit the headlines of the papers when they went far out; started to own business enterprises, married people by the hundreds in stadiums or stripped members of the right to visit their families.

All this has been going on probably since man started to form an organized group and a rival group proclaimed a better message.

Some of today's better-known magazines and newspapers belong to religious organizations. Quite an achievement, particularly on the part of groups who are not considered to be part of the mainstream religious organizations.

The Christian Science Monitor, a newspaper world renown, was started by Mary Baker Eddy. She was a visionary and created not only the newspaper but also a religious movement still in existence today.

Evangelists with the fervor to preach the gospel started their own churches, as did spiritualists who were not accommodated in their own denomination. "Spiritual Healers" went "underground" by organizing new churches to evade the law which protected the public from quackery.

Now "healing" could be performed as a religious ceremony without interfering with the medical profession. New groups, new churches, followers, believers...and of course the disenchanted.

Today's newspapers reflect in the church advertising the whole gamut of diversity, not only in Christianity but in all religious philosophies.

I decided to visit Spiritualist churches for a change.

Of course everyone must have heard about mediums who bring messages from the "dead". Having read the story of Houdini who in the latter years of his life devoted most of his time to debunk mediums, I was well prepared with skepticism. As far as mediums were concerned I was from Missouri and they had to show me.

The first church was a small chapel in the east end of the city.

A Scottish medium was advertised as the guest. I thought if any one comes all the way from overseas to show off their stuff in this country, well my expectations were high.

About 80 people turned out this Sunday to hear the message from beyond through a living person from faraway. I took a seat in the front row. After all I had heard of materializations, and other way-out phenomena and I wanted to see it up close.

Behind me the audience was made up of older folks, a relative term meaning in this case more persons in the congregation were over 60 years of age. Looking at them I felt a lot of expectation, a kind of anxiety on their faces. Some of them were troubled, which was obvious by just looking at them.

I would not class the people as poor, but somehow worldly riches did not seem to be in abundance, but then maybe these people did not want any. Maybe they had different priorities, who is to judge?

The chairs on the rostrum were taken by three ladies. One tall and lanky appeared to be the pastor, for want of a better word. None of the three had any of the colorful gowns catholic priests wear in services, neither did the three wear any identification like turbans or arm bands, just the regular street clothes, the same as the audience. It did not even look like Sunday clothing.

A hymn was announced and the three were identified. As I thought, the tall lady was the local leader, the short and stubby one the medium from Scotland and a "younger lady", around 40, was the local medium, also with a heavy Scottish accent.

Prayers, announcements, a short lecture about love, a collection, the reading of a list of people who needed prayer because of various illness—the finale was the medium.

By the way the collection basket appeared to be meager, mostly dollar bills, some change. My "Fiver" stuck out like a sore thumb, but it was too late to retrieve it when I noticed the usual giving. Maybe they don't want any more than a dollar, I thought.

Before the guest medium gave the performance, a few local "students" had the floor. They collected personal items like rings and chains and other items like pens and wallets and gave readings to the owners by clutching the item and talking about the feelings of the person.

"I have here a nice gold ring with a white pearl. The ring was given to the person as a present. It feels like a Christmas present. The owner of the ring has some family problems to contend with and there is an older vibration in the family circle who is very dominating and is creating pressure on the whole family. There is also another person in the family in need of medical attention......" some more information like that was given and then the medium asked "to whom does the ring belong?"

A white haired lady timidly lifted her arm, as everyone in the audience stared at her. "Me", she said.

"Did you understand the message?" the medium asked.

"Well, I think so", was the answer. The student medium selected another item.

It was called "Psychometry"; the reading of vibrations lodged on material items. The medium claimed that vibrations of the owners would stick to the items and that she could interpret these fine vibration emitted from the ring, wallet or pen.

The show went on.

Next was the local Medium with the Scottish accent. She was very confident in giving off some of the vibrations of the jewelry collected from the congregation.

The way she described a man's horseshoe ring with diamonds, I knew it was my turn. She had her eyes closed, her head in an upward position, as looking for help from the heavens. When she spoke it was fast and obviously, as far as she was concerned, without doubt.

"The ring feels hot in my hands, a lot of financial problems have come to the owner of this ring. There is a spirit guide here who announces that things will be the same for a while, as a situation has to be worked out through a learning experience.

"There is help for the financial situation. I see a three, that could mean three weeks or three months. I also see a lot of paper around this person, writings, letters, books, information, education"

"Who's is this?" The medium ask.

She was looking way in the back to the other side.

"Here," I said, "It's my ring, I think". She just handed me the ring, looked at me and said "I will see you later with a personal message".

I was intrigued.

Seeing books and magazines around me, well, I was in that kind of business, but could it have not applied to any one else in the audience. When you own a diamond ring, maybe you also own some books?

I could hardly wait for the personal message. The service went on and the guest medium finally took the podium.

She did not use psychometry, but just looked at a person or slightly pointed and nodded at one and asked "would you like a message" or something similar. She would then go right on talking.

Behind me sat an older gentlemen of about 70. His face looked friendly and kind. The medium talked to him.

"I have a lady here bringing you lot's of love my dear. She is your wife over on the other side. She is saying that the younger vibrations have their own life to live and not to worry that they won't be visiting that often. She is with you most of the time and she is telling me that you notice her quite often in the kitchen and in the garden. Those were her favorite places when she was on this earth plane. She is also sending love from your sister, who is also on her side. Sis wants you to remember the tree house and the wonderful time you had there with all your friends."

The medium paused briefly and tilted her head as if listening to a message from above. "Your wife tells me that you haven't been feeling well these last weeks and she wants you to buy some castor oil and rub those aching arm muscles with it. She also wants you to put aside those thoughts of joining her. It isn't time yet".

I looked around at the recipient of the message. He was nodding his head, a tear rolled down his cheek. His eyes were closed, his hands were folded as in prayer. He looked peaceful.

The medium brought messages to about ten more people. All receivers seemed to be able to identify with the information they got from beyond. She definitely made an impact on the congregation.

When she finished applause broke out.

Another prayer and the service ended; coffee and cookies were offered and everyone mingled. I looked for the medium to get the rest of my message. "You have to be careful of the legal papers you are signing", she said. "There is a paragraph which is not in your favor and will harm you if it is not renegotiated". She said that forewarned is forearmed.

While I was sipping my coffee and thinking about all that was going on around me, a man in his 50's with a bald head and gold rim glasses approached me. He gave me a piece of paper and just said "you will need this to understand". With that he turned around and left the room.

I looked at the paper. Three book titles and authors and the name of a local bookstore. It did not make sense, unless the man was the owner and wanted to peddle some books. I placed the sheet in my pocket and mingled with the congregation.

The medium from Scotland was surrounded by many people who wanted more information on their message, clarification. Some told her how "right on" she was with the information received. It was a very congenial group.

Everybody seemed to like each other, everybody happy, no arguments, no shouting, no complaining about wrong information, or that one could not identify with what was said.

There was a question I had to ask. After waiting my turn and exchanging small talk with members of the group I finally had a chance.

"How accurate is all the information you pass on and has anyone ever complained that the message was wrong?" I asked her.

"The information comes through my guide or from other entities beyond this plane, dear. Why should they be wrong? They have a different vantage point and can tell much more than we can. The odd time I may not interpret some of the symbols right, but I would say that 95% of all messages are right on."

Other people around me butted in and told me, that yes, she was very accurate in her readings.

I quickly asked "What did you do for a living before you got into this?"

"My dear man", she said very patronizing, "I don't give messages for a living. I am retired and I knew that I had the ability to see and hear more than other people, when I was a child. My job, well, before the war I was just a housewife, during the war I worked in a factory and after the war I became a nurse. Now I am retired and I pass on my gift to as many people as possible. I am teaching in a spiritualist church and develop mediums.

"Everybody has the gift, you know, just develop yours, I can see by your Aura, that you are very spiritual, you are a healer and you are a teacher yourself. Go to classes if you want to know more."

With that she turned to the cookie tray and marveled about the home baked stuff. Others got their turn to ask questions.

I was wondering what was wrong with the legal papers I had on my desk at home. The refinancing I had arranged for my business looked good to me. Tomorrow morning I was to meet with my lawyer and I was going to ask him—who knows, there may have been something in the message.

# 7

# *A Ouija board falls in to my hand.*

✦

## *This game scares me, despite the fact that it is only cardboard with a plastic pointer—*

While searching for some game boards in the toy store, the Ouija 'game' fell off the shelf, right into my arms.

I have read many books about the magical behavior of this "tool of the devil", by some beliefs but what could go wrong to try it just once?

On the back of the box the name was explained: Oui, French for 'yes' and ja, German for 'yes'.The board was bought and friends were invited for a party of fun and games. As the evening wore on and the regular games had been played, I told the story of a book I had just read, where some group had actually gotten a spirit from the other side to answer some questions by playing with the Quija board.

Disbelief was general consensus and I suggested trying it, as I had just bought the unit. My friends definitely recognized the manipulation attempt on my part. They agreed to give it a try despite my shameful behavior.

I sheepishly admitted, that I had second guessed them and was worried they would not play this game, as most religions scorn the use.

Nevertheless the game got under way and my punishment was that I had to wait until everyone else had its turn.

The pointer moved back and forth and someone in the group kept track of the letters and numbers and tried to make sense of it.

There seemed to be no special spirit in control and most of the time the players accused each other of moving the pointer across the board.

Finally I had my turn. My partner was a young lady by the name of Annie, who had come with a friend of mine. Annie was new in town and had never met any of the other participants. A bit shy, she hardly touched the plastic heart shaped indicator and my fingers were also just lightly placed on the side of the pointing heart.

The group was joking, as the results had so far been disappointing and I was quickly nicknamed "Dr. Faustus". I was encouraged to call on my master to get a message. It was in fun and nothing seemed to happen.

We decided to just move the pointer across the board, to get some motion going, not looking at the letters, just letting it flow.

Suddenly, the pointer was tearing away from my fingers, with my partners hand still on it, it briefly stopped at letters and the group called them out in unison, the scribe noted the letters and combined them to what seemed to be a message.

I had a hard time following and lost my place on the plastic a number of times. It just kept on going, the way it was described in the book I had read.

When it finally stopped it had spelled out

THIS IS YOUR MOTHER CALLING

We looked at the pad in amazement. Calling the letters, it was not immediately recognizable what the string of characters would mean, if anything. But now we were able to read it.

Everyone had a good laugh and teased me. They wanted to know how come that I was the one who's mother would come through. I objected.

"Why my mother, this could be any mother. How about Annie, she is my partner, maybe it is her mother?"

It was decided to keep on going to find out more about who's mother was giving us a message.

Annie and I placed our fingers into position and someone in the group asked "Who's mother are you, what is your name?".

Immediately the pointer started to move again and it slipped from under my hand again and only Annie was holding it with one finger, as the group called the letters in unison.

F R E D A

It stopped and we looked at the writing pad. My stomach seemed to go into butterfly motion. I asked Annie "is this your mother"?

She answered "no, and my mother is still alive anyway".

I looked around, everyone shook his or her head.

I got up—I did not want to play anymore.

My mother was on the other side. Her name is Frieda—and no one in this group could have known that, least of all Annie, who was holding the pointer alone for most of the letters.

# 8

## *Off to Mexico—on a vacation!*

*I can't get away from psychics; they follow me in to the hotel. But I didn't really want to make her cry—*

The jet touched down smoothly. We had arrived. Some passengers clapped. Mazatlan, Mexico.

I had never been here before and I hoped to spend a few days quietly in sunshine. Back home the snow season had started and it's good to get away from it and catch a tan.

The El Cid Hotel was luxurious. When you buy a package tour you somehow take your chances in selecting a hotel, but this one was first class, no question about it.

Going through the 'checking in', we retired for the rest of the night, after all, the plane landed at 1 am local time and the airport is more than a half an hour away from the beaches. Take another half an hour for check in, well, not much time left to sleep, when the maid knocks on the door at eight, because the "do not disturb" sign was not turned.

I strolled through the lobby after having a hearty breakfast and a poster caught my eye: "Psychic Reader".

A good looking blonde smiled at me from the photograph and the poster read "predicted Skylab....". Registration for appointments through the service desk of the hotel.

My curiosity could not bypass this one. It almost felt that I had come to Mazatlan to have a psychic experience. The appointment was made for the next day. Meeting the Psychic in the lobby of the hotel sharp at the agreed upon time was not typically Mexican. Well, neither was the Psychic.

She was tall, blond and good-looking. Her accent was more like Californian and as it turned out, she was born in the Midwest and moved and lived in Berkeley for some time, before making the journey to Mexico.

No, she was not wearing all the information on her forehead, but she was friendly enough to answer all my questions. We went from the lobby of the hotel to a room in the adjoining disco where she motioned me to a table. Some books and a tape recorder were the only accessories. It was in the afternoon, the disco was empty.

She started to talk about herself.

From the way she gave some calming explanations about a psychic Reading, I assumed that people are either scared when they look at a Psychic or this particular one has had some bad experiences.

She assured me that nothing out of the ordinary would happen; that psychic vibrations are all around us and that everybody could read them, if they wanted to.

It was a wordy explanation—definitely for a newcomer to the field. Since I did not interrupt and listened intensely, she must have thought that it was my first reading. Well it wasn't—but I was not about to tell her.

My background is journalism and one thing you learn when you are on the beat and listen to people: don't just believe everything they tell you. And in my search for psychic messages, I applied the same rules as I would in writing an investigative article for a newspaper or magazine—take nothing for granted, ask questions, don't assume—and be from Missouri.

The blonde was now ready to talk about me. She asked if I wanted the session recorded, if yes, an extra $2.00 was required for the tape. I agreed to buy the tape.The next fifteen minutes centered on something very strange for me. She talked about me, but she related to herself. Her experiences as a child; her father as an alcoholic; her quest for wanting to overcome shyness and low self esteem...she related it all to me and gave me plenty of advice as to how I could handle it for the better.

Another 10 minutes or so were spent on talking about my life at the present. But all I could get was a reading which anybody could have given to a North American tourist in Mexico, who obviously has enough money to spend to live in the El Cid, who will pay for a psychic, who is curious, reasonably educated and clean shaven...in other words, I got nothing unusual, nothing I could relate to as coming from the "other dimension". She mentioned, after asking if I was married, that my wife was not getting enough hugs, or something like that and that my daughter, after asking me whether I had children, would like to see more of me.

It was dribble, straight dribble and I couldn't stand it any longer. I interrupted and asked her if she could tell me something of my future. Well, she tried, but again dribble, nothing but dribble. No hard and fast facts. No extraordinary event, no forecast, no prediction.

I interrupted again and told her that I was actually disappointed.

I asked her if she could get something specific—she could not. Then I told her that I was a journalist and that I was going to write a book and asked if I could mention her in my book.

An earthquake could not have evoked a more dramatic reaction.

The word journalist must have done it. She cried, was upset that I "tricked" her and interrupted the tape immediately.

She told me that there was nothing in my future that I did not want to be there, that I was the type of person who would control the events around me and that she was very upset.

I wanted to pay for the session, but she would not let me. All she would take was the $2.00 for the half completed tape. She took her belongings and walked out of the disco.

To say that I felt bad, is an understatement. Anyone who knows me will agree, that the last thing on my mind is to upset good looking ladies. But all my sweet talk could not change her mind, she wanted to be upset and she was.

What else could I do, I went back to the room. On the way I passed by the poster in the lobby and looked at the picture again and decided that she was better looking in person than on the black and white photo.

At the beginning I had asked her how she had gotten into the psychic business and she told me about a dream she had some years ago. "I saw in my dream a space station falling down. The newspapers had reported that Skylab was returning to Earth and somehow I knew that the thing in my dream was Skylab."

"I also knew suddenly that it would land in Australia and the city nearby was Perth." Even as she recounted the story, she got excited. "I woke up and the dream was so vivid, that I knew it was a prediction. Somehow I had to warn some people. The first thing to come to mind was to phone the newspapers, the thought evolved in 'phone the newspaper in Perth, Australia'. I did just that.

"The editor on the other end was surprised. He ran the story and two days later the Skylab pieces dropped near Perth. A letter from the editor with a clipping of my prediction is still in my file".

She told me that after that experience her life changed. Excited about the possibilities of predicting the future she learned more about meditation and finer vibration until she was able to read people and help them in some of their predicaments.

My partner was in the room and without saying a word I grabbed my walkman and put the tape in. Half of the stereo headset I gave to her and I listened in. When it came to the abrupt stop I asked "What do you think?"

"She sure had you pegged right on", was the answer.I fell out of the bed.

# 9

# *Eastern philosophy has influenced the New Age movement. I had to go to India.*

## *I did not find "my Ashram" or "my Guru" but a fascinating country with fascinating people...and an American with insight*

Whenever I think of India, I have to make myself almost physically decide which India I want to zoom in on. You see India invokes some powerful pictures inside me. Four different 'India' offer themselves as choice.

I had done business with Indian companies before. The letters coming from that sub-continent were on paper very much different from our stationary. It never occurred to me to investigate exactly what the differences were, but just thinking about it now, I believe that it has something to do with the different kind of pulp used for paper making. Maybe the chemical process to whiten the paper is different, I don't really know.

From the letters I got another impression of the country, one of conservative business structure. All the correspondence sounded stilted in their English language, precise in their use of words...just different from letters I would receive from the continent or the British Isles. I could just imagine a conservative hierarchy within every business enterprise.

Then there was the picture of poor people living in the streets of Calcutta and suffering hunger pains. Mother Theresa came to mind and the many appeals for financial help on TV and Radio.

Another India was that of pomp and luxury. The traditional, historic India with castle and Maharaja, Tiger hunt and Elephant riding Sahib. Pages out of Rudyard Kipling.

And to top it off, the India of religious philosophy vied for attention. The Gurus, the temples, the burning bodies in the river, the festivals of light, the snake charmer and the Yogi.

Once I decided which India to think of, the pictures became quite clear and formed in line with my school training about the country and the many news stories and books I had read.

There was a nagging inside me to one day go and visit. To see for myself and to decide which India was the 'right' India. 'What should come to mind when the country's name was mentioned'?

I had to go—and I did.

In retrospect, I don't think any foreigner can know a country like India. Even living in the country for years one can only scratch the surface of the multifaceted India. Your experiences are shaped depending on the part of the land you lived in. It also would depend on which cast or culture you associated with. India is big and as the travel advertisements rightly claim: there is a lot to see.

My first encounter was with the political structure, the business in the capital city, the shopkeepers, the taxi drivers, the beggars and the crooks. After all, doing business in India as a foreigner—there is a lot to be learned. Not to get 'taken' becomes a goal.

But then, bargaining is a way of life. We think of set prices for commodities, in India, the price is what you are willing to pay for it and what the seller will let it go for. Not crooked, just time consuming and different from North America. Other cultures have similar traditions—nothing new.

The bureaucracy in India is something else. There are layers and layers of management with each group pushing it's own papers, having their own signing authorities and tax stamps. This is frustrating for someone wanting to do business in that country—as a foreigner. I spent weeks in various offices in New Delhi. There are ways around this. A few dollars in the right hand and the job gets done. Fast, efficient and without questions asked. To learn those skills is as important as producing a good product.

Maybe the government should do something about that. It sure would make it easier to do business there. Some call it corruption, some call it a way of life—some call it India.

From the center of the administration New Delhi, to the center of Commerce, Bombay. What a difference. There is a hustle and bustle about the latter city which can only be described as 24-hour activity.

Bombay never sleeps. Ships come from the Indian Ocean and the Arabian Sea to be loaded and unloaded. The harbor teems with modern trucks, old broken down trucks, donkey caravans, small motor driven cargo tricycles, human drawn rickshaw...a colorful twist worth watching.

On to Calcutta—poverty amongst the thousands and thousands of people living in the streets. Yes the TV pictures are right and yes, Mother Theresa's group and the many other western organizations who try to make a dent in the suffering need a lot of money to change anything.

There is only the question in the back of my mind, where is the help from the local wealth? There are some. There are a lot of them. Are they concerned as well, do they do their part to alleviate poverty?

Southern India, with beautiful beaches and different traditions could be a different country.

Looking at the mountains in the northern part one can not imagine that the heavy, sticky, humid and smelly environment of

Calcutta was in the same country. The fresh air is moving in from the snow covered peaks. The clear mountain lake where our houseboat was anchored to provide accommodation contrasts the brackish water of the southern rivers and bays.

Here people have other worries: Religious discrimination between Sikhs and Hindus; Rivalries between India and Pakistan and political concerns about China, just bordering in the north in the midst of the Himalaya. The way of life was different from the bigger cities in the south.

Outside of all the cities there is another India, people who make their living of the land. The farmers in rice paddies, wheat fields, nut plantations, wood lots....

Small villages with markets where the fruit of the land is sold are as colorful as the spices on display in open bowls. Exciting for the first time visitor. Picturesque.

I was looking for the Ashrams. Reading about some of the holy men who came from India to North America and made a fortune from their followers I needed to find the unspoiled Guru. The wise man who was going to convince me of his super natural powers—or wisdom. The Yogi who was going to demonstrate his contempt for his body by burning it and only living in the spirit (maybe this was a bit much to ask).

The God men were easily recognized by their robe. The special colorful cotton sheet wound around their body and the shaven head signified that the person had given their life to Rama, Siva, Buddha or.... I talked to many of them.

Communication was sometimes difficult but my travel companion/guide could translate many of the local dialects and I could get a good idea of the various philosophies and religious variations these people taught to their listeners.

Ashrams the way I envisaged them I did not see. Yes, I visited the famous schools, filled with American students and European followers. All organized in a way that would make General Motors proud.

I also visited way out of the way colonies of monks who devoted their life to the studies of the mysteries. No foreigners here.

Little schools could be found in many of the market places where followers of a holy man sat in a circle and listened to the story he had to tell.

Some of the stories were based on the teaching of the Buddha. Some were brought down through the ages and now printed in the Bhagavad-Gita. Some of the stories were secret knowledge given to the master through some grand masters in the monasteries or through visitors in spirit.

Is one year too short to study the people, the religion the way of life? Of course. Ten years? Yes—It will take a lifetime to understand. And then some more life times to come back and grow.

The wheel of life is slow and cumbersome.

In one of the hotels in a medium sized town was a table with a tent card and small banner: Indian Horoscope by expert! Leave your name and room number.

What could be more enticing than to investigate an Indian horoscope. My name and room number went into the guest book on the table. I noticed a lot of American and German names as I flipped through the back pages. I am sure that was a 'no no'!, Well, research needs investigation and clarification. I already had my doubts about the Astrologer, not even knowing what an Indian Horoscope was all about.

My doubts came simple from observing the other holy men who sort of lived off the land by asking the people they told stories to, to contribute to their living. And the people did. They gave spices, food and other things of value. Seldom did I see money exchanged for the services supplied. This could mean that the listeners did not have any or that the holy man did not want any.

The Hotel Astrologer had his price: $ 50. US (sic) currency.

I was in the midst of eating my Tandoori Chicken as the dining room waiter brought me a little note: "Your appointment with the Astrologer is right after dinner in the lobby."

He was dressed in traditional Indian cotton cloth and he was sitting next to his table on an upholstered chair. He beckoned to me to do the same.

He appeared to go into a short meditation as he closed his eyes. Then he asked me about my birthday. I told him.

Again silence.

He then started to speak and gave me some insight into my character. Told me about my family, my desires, my past experiences. I was impressed. A lot of the information I could relate to.

Then I was asked to pose some questions to him.

I had one very much burning in my mind. "Where did he learn his English?" He had spoken to me in English and it was not the typical Indian dialect but more a Midwestern American slang that came out of his mouth. And sure enough he told me that he went to school in Chicago. This really baffled me.

Forgetting the request that I was to ask questions about my future life, I interviewed him about himself. He was willing to answer and his life story was actually very interesting.

His family lived in San Francisco when he was born. They had moved there from Fiji. When he was 10, his father started an accounting firm in Chicago and the family moved. After military service which got him to Germany and Guam he decided to study some of the family's background and traced their roots back to India.

While doing that he also studied Astrology with a German-American. He made some money with charting horoscopes for people.

He then got involved with a group, which worshipped a young Indian cult leader. At one time, he had to accompany a group of followers to India were they were going to build a resort to invite Americans to study the cult philosophy.

Somehow he felt that the group was not for him and he returned to the States and started counseling people through astrology, making a few dollars on the side. He worked as a commercial artist in a publishing house in his full time job.

One day he decided to go back to India and to live there. He said it was difficult at first, because he was really an American.

Some of his former Astrology customers kept in touch with him and actually sent him new business: Friends and Relatives.

From his Wiesbaden military days, he still had friends in Germany and he kept contact with them as well and from here too business started flowing in.

"Today, I am doing well", he said. "I get a lot of letters from my customers, telling me how good I forecasted their future. That helps to increase business."

There was one more question I wanted him to answer.

"When you requested my birthday, you did not ask me for the town I was born in. Don't you need to know that in order to calculate the star constellations?" I asked.

He pondered the question for a while and then started off with a sigh:

"You are the first who asked me that question and I don't want to lie to you."

There was a dramatic pause before he continued.

"You see, I don't really construct the astrological houses. When I was in the group I told you about, we did a lot of meditation. One day I was thinking about my girl friends birthday and suddenly around the dates I saw a lot of mental pictures. Pictures which appeared to be in the future as well as in the past. There was a dividing line and I could tell the difference.

Also I could see the pictures who meant absolute fulfillment as very clear and some pictures were fuzzy, like the action in those could be changed."

He paused again.

"I talked to my friend about the pictures and she was amazed. I had told her accurate facts from the past and we both were going to monitor the future".

Well, he did find out that the future too was accurate. And that some of the fuzzies really could be changed, if she wanted to change them.

Some more meditation and some more tests with other birthdays gave him the confidence that this was something he could do well.

"I got married to my friend and we lived for a while together but somehow it did not work out. She always wanted me to look into her future. She build her whole life around my pictures. She was never herself. We got a divorce."

He then decided to go back to India and set up shop in this hotel, which was frequented by American tourists traveling the country side, like myself.

"I would be pleased if you would not think of this as false advertising", he said "because Astrology is meaningful to the tourists and the birth date is the key which unlocks the information, I don't think that I am doing anything wrong, even though I know it is not the traditional Astrology I am working with. In any case, I call it 'Indian Astrology'".

I was amazed and paid my dues gladly.

He declined my invitation to tea or beer to talk some more and just smiled and waved.

"You better make notes of our conversation", he said, "your book article on me should contain all the facts".

"Was that a fuzzy picture or a clear one", I queried jokingly. He answered in the same vain: "A very clear picture"

# 10

## *Finding the fountain of youth in a sports car.*

✦

### *Spiritualist churches seem to draw people with new ideas. Can a tiny wheat germ really influence your age?*

Her carbody was constructed of fiberglass throughout and appeared to be made from one of those do-it-yourself kits. It sure attracted attention everywhere. Mind you, so did the lady.

When I first met her, it was in a parking lot of a spiritualist church, which had a "psychic day". I was going to look over the mediums and add to my collection of names and addresses of people in the business.

As she got out of the car she was balancing a parcel and the light wind seemed to get caught in her open jacket, making a balloon out of it and destabilizing her walk.

I offered my help that was gladly accepted. We both headed in the same direction.

Once inside, I placed the parcel on a table and heard the sound of glass. "Some jars of marmalade or pickles" I thought to myself as there was a bake sale after the psychic event.

The lady thanked me and introduced herself with her first name. I did likewise and she asked me whether I wanted to buy some. "Buy what"? I asked. "The jars you carried in", she replied.

She must have noticed my confused look on my face, as she said, “Oh you did not look inside, go ahead and look”.

Well I did not buy. What I had carefully carried to the church from the parking lot were jars labeled ‘wheat germ’. In various forms, juice, green, white…yak.

I did the polite thing and asked what it was good for and she rattled out the names of organs who would appreciate the wheat germ. In addition, she pointed out “it keeps you young and beautiful”. She smiled as she said that and I smiled back. That one I had heard before. Even though I must admit that, she did look young and beautiful, but then when women are in their late twenties they do look like in their prime—to me anyway.

There were some good mediums at the event and I interviewed a number of them. Time flew by and before I knew it the bake sale started. I walked over to a long table where lots of cookies and salads and pickles and things were offered. “Funny bake sale”, I commented pointing to the many non-baked items—among them wheat germ.

The ladies selling the stuff just smiled. “Anything to raise funds for the church—to pay the rent”, an elderly matron lectured me.

My acquaintance from the parking lot was behind the table too. She pointed to her wheat germ cookies and guaranteed me that they were baked. Her grandson liked them—I would too.

“Whose grandson?” came my query, as I thought she was about to joke with me but she smiled and proudly answered “mine”.No, I was not about to go blind or lose my judgment of women—I did not believe her. Some quiet enquiries with one of the other attendants confirmed however, that the lady had a grandson. Not adopted, not a fluke of nature—she was over 50 years old. I could not believe my eyes and kept on staring at her, to the point that it became embarrassing to meet her eyes, but I could not help myself.

Later on in the evening, I asked her about the wheat germ. Did it really help her to stay young? “You better believe it”, she said.

I learned from another lady who must have noticed my undue staring that not only did the wheat germ keep her young, but also alive, as she had an illness which the doctors had pronounced terminal.

Some medium had given her a message from a spirit uncle that she should grow her own wheat and prepare it in a special way.The recipe was given as well, it would keep her alive and beautiful.Well, it sure did, the message was given to her over 10 years ago.

# 11

# *The universal job bank is calling*

◆

***The young man sang 'praise the Lord' so loud, he stood out in the crowd of older parishioners.***

There was the feeling that I needed to meet the man who had been singing the hymns so loudly. He was sure of himself and looked like he had it all together. Even his name suggested royalty as I found out later.

It was coffee time after the church service and I ambled to him with cup in hand, crunching on some home made goodies. (Church auxiliaries always seem to know how to bake). After the usual chit chat—in spiritualist churches it goes like "good vibration here tonight" or "excellent healers in this church" or "good message service"—I ask outright "What are you doing for a living?"

The answer came promptly. He was a salesman.

I tried to convey as politely as I could that he was sort of sticking out of the crowd—he looked more prosperous and, well, better educated than the rest of the people.

He was. But, getting details out of him was not easy.

It took an invitation for coffee and a chat in the nearby restaurant to get more information about him. He explained it in simple terms.

"I was down and out", he confessed, "when I first came to this church. My career was gone, my friends disappeared—I was depressed. That was when I looked for a church to get some answers and maybe consolation."

The rest of the story was similar to ones I would hear over and over again.

At first they would try the established church. The one their parents belonged to; the one they were christened in. No one would help or even find the time to listen to the problems. Many laid blame on them and promised punishment and absolution.

Then there would be the search for a psychic. What is in store for me tomorrow? That would lead to a spiritualist church and here the real miracle would take place.

The people were friendly, did not judge and believed that the spirit forces, the universal spirit or the spirit within you (depending on the group) would heal you. They would believe in laying-on of hands for problems like "I don't have a job" or "How can I get some money to buy some food".

There would be spiritual rallies where the mediums would tell them what would happen tomorrow—next week—next month. It appeared that most of the messages fell on fertile ground. In the discussion afterwards people would tell the medium how good they were in examining the past and present—and how, hopefully their predictions for the future would turn out accurately—if the message was positive.

This was one of the strange things. Nowhere did I hear that Aunt Nellie was going to pass over tomorrow. Nobody talked about the leg breaking next week—but somehow those messages were given. couched in words like "A vibration near you wants to learn more of the other side and is contemplating leaving this body. Spirit says that changes may be made, that it may take some time for everyone to adjust to the new situation." Then there would be an upbeat message, which would make it all O.K. to the person receiving the information.

Sometimes I would see tears running freely. People knew exactly what was meant.

The broken leg was announced as "Watch your step, you have been saying lately that you are overworked and that you need some rest. Spirit is listening and is planning on fulfilling your wishes to give you more time to study".

Yes my newly made friend got consolation from the messages. The positive environment, the friendliness of the people got him involved in doing some work for the church. It felt good around the mediums and the healers. He felt good about himself.

Did he get back on his feet? Of course. A medium told him not to take the job offered to him within three days but to wait for a letter to come and accept the lower paying proposition, as it would turn out for the better.

I was curious, what happened?

"A job offer came over the phone on the third day. One of the many resumes I had mailed panned out. The personnel manager on the other end of the phone sure got a shock when I told him, that I would pass this opportunity. He even offered more money. But I said no. Mind you I was shaking in my boots. Here was a possibility to get back to work and I said no. I had been looking for a long time and could not even get close to an offer. It was like I was out there in the corner, watching this guy—me—say no to the job."

The next day he got an offer in the mail with more money, better advancement opportunities and all kinds of perks on top of it.

He had stepped out in faith—and came through. No wonder he was singing so loudly "praise the Lord".

# 12

# *Order a steak, well done, with a psychic message on the side.*

◆

## *Discussing channeling over dinner may not be everyone's fare but sure makes me curious*

The lady owns a restaurant and every time we go there for dinner she joins us at the table. She is well spoken, well dressed and in general a nice person, whatever that may mean.

Just when the subject comes to psychic phenomena or spiritual healing, she becomes very "knowing" and speaks with authority.

Whose authority? Some entity she channels to give her the truth on worldly matters as well as spiritual matters.

This can be a traumatic experience for someone not used to dealing with unseen beings, spiritual guides or masters of the white brotherhood.

One day we talked about a woman who owns a ranch in the North-West and is taken over by a 35000 year old entity. She has become famous by now. A movie star talked about her in a book and with all kinds of publicity—bingo, the crowds came to the ranch and the money started to roll in.

I had seen some tapes of the lectures where the entity takes over the body of this good looking lady and starts to speak in a foreign accent, doling out wisdom from beyond.

Being from Missouri, I stood my ground and argued against the authenticity of those demonstrations, after all, I had not seen them in person and in any case what did the entity tell us that was not known before, preached in the Bible, the Torah or could be found in the Koran or books of Eastern wisdom?

My dinner companion and the restaurant owner were convinced that the messages given by the lady/cum entity/cum man were true. To convince me they made me promise to watch some tapes of a public lecture and to find a prediction or a truth which would change my mind.

I did watch.

Laughingly I pointed to a session in the tape where the entity talked about Russia. She/he predicted that the Russian people would soon be more democratic than the USA citizen, or something like that.

This was my cue. I know the Marxist/Leninist philosophy. Democracy is a dirty word in their camp. I told my friends exactly that and finished the subject matter.

The restaurant owner is still channeling and getting her truth from beyond; my friend is still listening to the 35000 year old and somehow now, after some time, some of the things they are saying ring true.

I decided then, that one day I would go and see for myself—Then I would prove to my friends that it was all nonsense.

There is only one nagging thought in the back of my mind? The channels predicted environmental changes, medical breakthroughs and behavior changes—long before it was popular to be concerned about them. Long before the governments of the world decided to do anything about pollution, recycling or restricting production of pollutants.

And about that democratic Eastern Block—well, things have happened that I would not have dreamed of a many years ago.

While I had decided to see the "entity", I also paid more attention to the restaurant owner's predictions. After all, her channel gave out some information which still sound ridiculous today—maybe they are true tomorrow?

We discussed channels coming through automatic writing as in the books of Ruth Montgomery and channels coming through a person in trance, as in the case of Edgar Cayce, the transmedium giving health information to thousands of people with an astonishing success rate. Whatever is channeled through some ordinary person becomes profound information to which the medium did not have access through their past education.

It is hair raising, just to think about it.

Even though I am a skeptic at heart, my open mind is opening wider.

# 13

# *The Warrior incarnates after 35000 years.*

## *The body looks youthful, blond and female—the spirit speaking is old, wise, expensive and male*

It was a powerful entrance. 500 people screaming and applauding, the music in loud disco fashion filling the hall with a sound of a thousand drums.

There, in a white dress, blond hair and striding towards the podium was the 35,000 year old entity 'Ramtha'(a registered trade mark) with a borrowed body.

It was hard for me to believe that I was part of this group. Looking around I found only enthusiastic followers happy to see this person. Was I the only skeptics? Who knows? I was definitely the only one taking notes of the event as a journalist, I think.

Cameras and recording devices were not allowed. A notice to that effect said, that film and camera would be seized. This show was copyrighted and the organizers sure knew how to protect their investment.

Just a few years back I had heard for the first time about this being. He apparently borrowed a body from a vivacious young lady, who went by the name of 'JZ', and started to preach messages about the world; the past; the future.

He would predict and manifest for friends—in other words, a convenient fellow to have around. Except that JZ claimed that she was "out" when he was "in". That somewhat shortened her life and reading the biography of the JZ, she told the entity at one time to take a hike, so to speak.

Obviously the situation changed. JZ provided the real estate and the organization as well as her body. The entity Ramtha kept on preaching and the followers grew in numbers—and spiritually according to them.

Today, a whole business empire sells anything from T-shirts to tapes, films to books—and the seminars. "Personal" appearances by the entity are not really cheap. It is structured like a school—a 'school of enlightenment', based on 'Gnostic' or hidden knowledge. There are scheduled classes and impromptu events. You can not fail the school, as long as you are registered as a student and attend the mandatory classes.

It all happens at a ranch in the Northwest. Located in a small town, the area is overrun by tourists and seekers. After all, a glimpse of Ramtha, the warrior, and maybe a personal message could change your life.

In the meantime, JZ has to live in the community and cope with the ever-lasting question "is she telling the truth or is this a wonderful act?"

Some of the critics who are more into psychology and psychiatry have labels for the behavior and point to literature where having multiple personalities is described as a disorder.

The religious community points to the Bible and wishes they could get a priest to exorcise her. Bible thumpers are convinced that she is possessed of the devil.

New age seekers find in her a channel proclaiming the truth and the second coming of Christ. JZ in her own personality is charming, bright and feminine. In the role of Ramtha, she appears more masculine. Her stride, her gestures, her body language in general is definitely 'male'.

Channeling has become popular and specialty stores are filled with books, audio- and video tapes, of mediums who announce anything from the white brotherhood to special spiritual entities, known or unknown in the past. Judging by the magazines who report on all the happenings—business is booming.

This school is a bit different though, JZ got a group of experts to wire her up and observe her bodily and mental functioning during a channeling session. Apparently, these professionals had no doubt that something 'unusual' is going on in JZ's body. With that confirmation, even the locals take a different look at the hoopla which is going on at event time. It helps of course that all those students from all over the world leave a lot of coin in the town.

And then of course the biggest suckers are the skeptics. Having to keep an open mind, they have to go and investigate all the various entities and judge their performance by themselves. They don't even get a break from the organizers and have to pay full price.

I had paid the full price.

Armed with knowledge from some of the publications and video tapes of the entity, some predictions, and also armed with some knowledge about JZ, putting on the show, I was looking for the slip up.

The teaching was good. Spiced with quotations from the Bible and other publications, accepted as the foundation of some of the religious philosophies, there was nothing new in that message. The messenger was new and the way it was explained was new.

"You have the power over your personal reality". Why are you complaining? Change your reality.

It felt to me like an introduction into hermetics. The entire secret teachings are now revealed in easy to understand words.

"Life is not real—it changes". You make the changes.

The ancient schools of wisdom had come back to open the vault to the listener.

"Consciousness and Energy creates the nature of reality". (This may be a copyrighted phrase).

I really had to write fast and listen at the same time to get the gist of the matter. It all made sense: "Nothing is were the something's come from".

Of course writing this now, as tidbits of the teaching, is unfair, I realize that. But I want you to understand the kind of messages brought forward in the seminar. The kind of teaching, which is accepted now, as it comes in a different package.

I remember struggling over "God is spirit" way back in Sunday School and when I was to understand that "God is within".

Ramtha droned: "Consciousness and Energy creates the nature of reality in between lives". All of it was explained. It all made sense too, when one realizes that some of our physicists could change their mind tomorrow about the current teachings in our Universities.

But then, that too has been happening throughout the ages. Our science is being updated as we go along. Who says, that the entity could not be right 10 years from now? Lucky the believer who acted already today.

The hall we were in was actually a riding hall. The wood chips and the turf were still on the ground. We had been asked to bring sleeping bags and water, as well as box lunch to make ourselves comfortable.

Throughout the weekend, I had a feeling that the message was ok. Having been exposed by now to other occult teachings, there was nothing new. I was just a bit uncomfortable about the messenger. His (or her) truth included the standard doom and gloom predictions about earthquakes, floods and draughts. There was the suggestion to move to the country side, as the air in the cities would be too polluted. And there was the comforting connotation that it was ok if one did not follow any one of the remedies.

In one way or the other, the end of the world has been predicted by many spiritual leaders. References in the Bible, the verses of Nostradamus, messages from UFO contacts—at one time most of the famous prophets and psychics predicted the disappearance of the world (the way we know it). This entity was not any different.

There were suggestions that the God inside us can materialize gold and things; matter of fact another course was teaching specifically that. The right spiritual attitude was most important though. Be happy.

Happy was the crowd around me, I must say. Everyone enjoyed the uplifting suggestion that we can and will change the things around us, things that bother us. For the weekend at least none of the troubles of the past showed in the group.

We were instructed in breathing, power breathing. We had to sit in the lotus posture, called triad position—it was at times back-breaking to keep up the position for any length of time. But happiness prevailed.

The sincerity of the medium, the love evoking message, the group dynamic and last, but not least, the promise of a better tomorrow—it all made it seem ok. Why not listen and learn. Why not give it the benefit of the doubt.

Many a person will materialize their desires after the seminar. We know that a burning desire coupled with an attitude of believe will move mountains.

As for myself, I had studied many of the tapes from earlier seminars with predictions which should have come through by now. The result—well, on some the jury is still out. Some have come through and some may have just had the wrong date attached to them.

I intend to go back one day and ask for an individual interview, if that could be arranged.

With psychic predictions no one will ever know for sure, unless it is proven to the individual. And I am no exception.

There is only one thing that bothers me. While listening to the tapes from 20 years earlier, Ramtha predicted that the "people of the land of the bear" (Russia) would be more sovereign than the people of this country".

At the time this prediction was uttered we lived in a world of two great powers in a cold war. Knowing the communists, there was no way, in my opinion, that they would change their attitude to give their people more freedom—more sovereignty.

It was even impossible to imagine that the populous would demonstrate and asked for democracy, given the example of Hungary, Czechoslovakia and East Germany in the past, were tanks and machine guns squelched any demand for liberty.

Seeing the development in the former communist countries now, and our own security measures placed on our people, I must give credit to Ramtha for a daring prediction.

Was it a lucky guess or does Ramtha really know the future and all there is to know?

# 14

# *The spirit doctor from Vienna won't help me quit smoking.*

✦

***He could convince some, but not all; particularly since he could not speak German—***

He was supposed to be a trance-medium. His guide was a medical Doctor from Vienna who passed over to the other side of life around 1910. A colleague in the office had met him and had arranged to have another meeting in the evening.

Knowing that I was researching the unexplained, she invited me to come along. I was excited.

On the way to the east end of the city our conversation revolved around the medium. I tried to find out from my colleague as much information as possible. Being prepared was half the battle in evaluating psychic phenomena.

We rang the bell at a commercial building in a strip plaza. There were retail shops with apartments above all along the street. A young lady opened the door and led us downstairs into the basement of a shop.

For a moment my mind flashed pictures of séances through my head. Many of those I had only read about, some of them I had attended.

The setting I was walking into could have been right out of a book.

The room was very dark and only after a while could I distinguish the other people around me. A candle flickered as I was directed towards a chesterfield. I sat down. It felt like an old chesterfield, with the springs making themselves uncomfortably known.

My colleague sat next to me. Some faces could now be distinguished, particularly two smokers lit themselves up whenever they took a drag on their cigarette. A conversation was carried between three people. They were talking about a medical condition of a lady who had received a reading by the spirit Doctor.

There were eight people in the room. The candle was in the centre and some sofas and chairs had been arranged in somewhat of a circle.

An elderly lady announced that we all had arrived and that the service would start. Service? This was new to me. Why would they call it a service? I was soon enlightened.

Let us pray, the lady said and started with the Lord's prayer. We all fell in murmuring the words. Then a tape recorder was engaged to play a gospel hymn. Again, everyone hummed the tune and some even knew the words. Then came a request for donations. A basket made the rounds. A $10 bill at the bottom made a strong suggestion. When I passed the basket to the left I had put my $10 in as well. Now I understood the "service".

We then were told that the medium, her husband, was going to invoke the Doctor, I forgot his name. It sounded very German. Her husband then prepared himself by breathing heavily. During the earlier conversation I had heard him talk and somehow thought that I had detected a slight Scottish accent with him.

I don't know why I somehow got the feeling that I had donated ten dollars to a not so good cause. My gut told me to beware. Not that I was asleep, because I wanted to check this one out and usually everyone gets the benefit of the doubt until proven otherwise. I thought that was just fair.

In this case, I felt taken.

I asked my colleague for a cigarette. She looked at me strangely, knowing that I had quit the habit many years ago. I motioned for her to give me a light as well. She did.

"Gutten Abend meine Freunde. It is verry nice to hawe you heere".

The medium spoke. Except for the introductory greeting he spoke English with a German accent and I mean German, not Austrian, which is usually softer than the guttural Hochdeutsch.

Dr. X spoke of the many wars in this world which were bad news for the spirits on the other side. They did not like what they were seeing. He also spoke of the many spirit guides who were here tonight to help him. He predicted many healings like in the olden days when he was here on earth.

The lady intervened and asked him whether he had messages for the group. He affirmed. "Tonight wwee vill haff goot messages".

Everyone was going to get one, plus a healing.

He turned to a middle aged man next to him and told him about his leg which was healing well and that he was pleased that his prescription to drink a certain tea was being followed. "I can schmell it", he said pointing to a cup in front of the subject.

A young lady was asked next what her chest condition was doing. It appeared that the doctor was talking to his regular clientele.

I asked my colleague for another cigarette.

My turn came after Dr. X gave a prescription to the young lady which contained a lot of water drinking and some chest rubbing instructions.

"Vat can I do for you jung mann?", he asked looking in my direction.

In slow, easy to understand words I told him, in German, that I wanted to stop smoking. Could he please help me?

"Ja, Ja", he mumbled and said "Alles gut".

With that he turned to my colleague and said to her that he had noticed that she had fallen into very bad influences. She should watch out not to be misled.

On he went to the next lady.

I snubbed my cigarette.

Many years ago I had watched "Hogan's Heroes" on TV and our medium reminded me very much of "Schultz". I was wondering if the accent I was hearing did not originate with the show.

There were a few more German words thrown into the conversation. "Fraulein", he called his wife and "danke, danke" he said once to another lady.

So far I had not spoken with anyone else there. I decided to keep it that way to the end. Let them think that I can't speak English, I thought.The session ended. A prayer of protection was offered by the master of ceremonies. Coffee and tea was offered for anyone who wanted to stay.

I did not.

My colleague was upset. "What did you say"?, she asked when we were in the car.

"That he should help me to quit smoking", I said.

"But you don't smoke".

"That is the point."

Only then did she understand.

She went back to the medium the following week and told them what I had done. Up to then they did not realize that I had tested the medium but they sure were upset when they heard the story. They asked her never to come back.

The message to her, while we were there, was concerning her boyfriend who had gotten into the alcohol. That was why she had visited the 'Doctor' in the first place. She had told him the whole story. His advice the first time around was to leave her boyfriend and come back to a séance for more direction.

Some direction, some medical advice, some Austrian doctor.

# 15

# *Another church—another psychic.*

✦

## *Can they read my mind or do they really get information from spirit?*

While doing my research, there were many more churches on my list and some of them I left in the middle of the service. Boring, uninspiring, just a handful of people in the congregation—I could not see me wasting my time.

Some of the churches only existed because someone who had nothing better to do and wanted to be of service to the community kept the doors open.

Others were nothing better than a social club for people to come and chat.

While this is a noble goal for the people involved, there was no extraordinary spirit present, to warrant investigation. Just another dead church.

One of them was in the west end of town and the Saturday evening meeting was advertised as a healing service.

I was there, sitting among 40 others, mostly of "golden age". The preacher was a woman and while she gave the sermon, she closed her eyes and preached about one of the letters of Paul.

My mind had been made up, that I would leave right after the collection, because there seemed to be again nothing unusual going on.

And I had made it a rule for myself, that whenever I would visit a church, I would give some money into the basket. Why?—Well, maybe to pay the rent for my chair, maybe to help them to keep on going—maybe.... I don't really know.

As the announcements came from the rostrum, just before the offering, the preacher pointed at me and said "Welcome to our little church".

I was a bit embarrassed, as all heads turned to me. I nodded quietly and fumbled the money in my hand. She went on to say "You have to stay to experience the healing service, before you write about our church".

My head went up in shock. I looked at her. How did she know that I was planning to write? How did she know that I was just about to leave?

Again, I nodded my head and looked down. My heart was pounding.

The singing was awful. One man carried the tune loud and added fancy side notes. The pianist, with her big hat, played like in a concert and the rest of the congregation just tried to be polite without raising their voice. The preacher lady did not sing, but sat with her eyes closed before a huge cross.

A collection basket made the rounds. Dollar bills were dominant. My Five seemed to be out of place.

After the hymn the lights went out and four candles were lit. "We are now coming to that part of our service where we ask the holy spirit to come down and heal our bodies," said the preacher.

Some stools had been arranged in front of the altar. Three persons from the congregation, the pianist and the preacher stood behind the stools, eyes closed, arms stretched out, palms directed upwards.

People stood up and went to stools to sit down. The one behind laid the hands on different parts of the body of the person. I could guess that here the spiritual healing was invoked and that the people on the stool were going to be healed of whatever ailed them.

After about 5 minutes the healers would go to a wash basin and wash their hands, while the "healed" person would go back to their pew. Then the healer would again stand behind the stool and someone else would come up to sit down.

The procedure was repeated until the stool stood empty.

Another person went to the podium and read a list of names to be included in our prayers. They called it "absent healing". The list was impressive. At least 30 names were on the list. It sounded like the whole congregation was sick.

A Psalm was said in unison and then the lights were back on.

Another song, just as awful as the others and then coffee, tea and cookies in the back room.

I ambled over there and grabbed a coffee. The preacher noticed me and came to shake my hand.

"Welcome again", she said. "This is all new to you, but you will get used to it."

With that she turned to another lady and hugged her "Good to see you back on your feet again. We had a special healing service for you last Wednesday. Spirit obviously is working."

She turned once more to me and said "Enjoy the fellowship, we will see you again—and keep up the good work".

"Do you know the Reverend?" The question came from the man with the loud singing voice.

"No", I said, "this is my first time here".

"I know that", he said "but I had the feeling that she knew you from before. Matter of fact, I think that you traveled in a past life together. Maybe you are even soul mates".

He turned and mumbled something and got himself a tea.

Another lady spoke to me and made me feel welcome. She insisted that I try her rice cookies. "I made them today, they are fresh. Just have one." She was right, they were fresh and delicious. I took a second piece. The lady beamed.

"You must make sure that you cut some of your cholesterol intake", she said, "otherwise you are a healthy person. You have good spirits around you and I like your colors in your aura". She smiled and turned away.

Strange, I thought, just this morning I had a medical check up after 5 years not seeing a Doctor. The only thing he told me was to cut the creamer out of my coffee—'that will be enough to balance your cholesterol'.

I was amazed. At that moment I decided to come back to this church at a later date.

# 16

# *It's all in your handwriting*

## *Your next letter may reveal the future, or past, to someone in the know—*

A lady who was a friend of a friend was supposed to be able to interpret handwritings. I was game to test her skills. It needed two pages of written stuff and two weeks to wait for the results.

Because the lady did not know me in person, I felt confident that whatever she detected in the scribbles of mine would be true interpretation and not something she got to know by hanging around me.

Once I got her report I was prepared to tear it apart and to write about it as a pseudo science which belongs right in the category of tea leaf readings and crystal ball gazing.

Reading the first paragraph I thought, 'the lady is clever'. She was giving me all those good attributes I could not argue with. After all I thought of myself too as caring and feeling and being diplomatic.

But it went on to say that I had a keen mind and "...fluidity, which is the ability of the mind to move easily and smoothly from one subject to another. It is also a sign of creative thinking".

This lady got me.

The next pages described me very well. Even some of my attitudes were laid open as if there was no hiding place for my deepest and darkest secrets.

What really astonished me was a comment almost at the end: "you are probably careful about what you eat".

Now this may be a statement suitable to everyone who reads this but it was strange for me to see it there. I was an original food junkie. I liked to eat what I wanted to eat. Never thought of dieting or eating regular meals at regular times.I even called myself a sandwich freak, because those were my favorites.

Now, only a week before I had written the test pages, I had looked at myself and while still liking what I saw, I thought I could do away with that spare tire around my waist. It was then that I decided to keep an eye on the food I would take in. And it was then that I decided to eat some green stuff as well. Up to this time the mere thought of a bowl of salad was horrifying to me.

Reading the report over again I must say that there must be something in my handwriting which reveals my personality to a total stranger. And if handwriting analyses can do it, maybe aura reading can do it—maybe cards—maybe tea leaves?

# 17

## *My book list comes back to haunt me.*

◆

### *Is there such thing as a "Mystic"? And what is "Reality" anyway?*

The last thing on my mind was a spiritual church. It was a relaxing weekend for me and strolling along the downtown store fronts I was reminded on inflation—as I saw the price tags in the windows—and our culture in general when I looked at the peddlers on the side walk and the bums hustling for change.

"How are you today?"

The voice was a deep pleasant sounding tenor close to my ear. I turned around and smiling from ear to ear was the gentleman I had met in one of the churches. He was the one who had given me the list with books and the name of the book store.

"Hi !", I answered just as cheerfully, "how are you doing?", still surprised that he even recognized me. We stood in front of a jewelry store and exchanged pleasantries.

His bald head was shining as if recently buffed and the gold rimmed glasses were the same he had worn in the church.

He was in a hurry. He had to pick up his airline tickets to fly to Austria.

"By the way", he said, "you have lost the list of the books I gave you and I thought I should write them down again."

With that he pulled a piece of paper out of his shirt pocket and handed it to me. At the same time he held out his hand, shook mine and said "I will be back in 4 weeks time, we will be in touch then."

He turned and walked down the street, with me looking perplexed at the paper. It almost looked like the very same piece I was once given by him. The same titles and the same book store.

Yes, I had lost the paper. Just recently it came to my mind and I looked for it, but it must have gone with the many old newspapers and magazines I had put out for the Boy Scout recycling campaign.

How did this fellow, I still did not know his name, knew that I had lost the paper?

Did he carry the list around with him, speculating, that one day he would meet me.

I looked at the paper, it looked to clean to be hanging around someone's shirt pocket for too long.

Was he pushing these books to anyone and did he have dozens of those pieces of paper in his pocket?

This whole thing puzzled me.

My next stop was the book store on the list and I browsed through the many titles. The shop was specialized and only carried "new age" stuff, religious and philosophical books.

Some of the volumes looked like they were published around the turn of the century—but still new.

I got the attention of a clerk and I showed him the list.

"Sorry, but the first one has to be ordered, the rest is here".

'Might as well go for it', I thought and ordered the first book, which would take about one week for delivery. The others I bought too and the shock I got from the price tags was something else.

"We don't sell many of them, they are just for people who know." was the answer to my question 'who else would be buying this type of books'?

One title was about color energy, another about sound vibration and their energy and how it effects the human body. The book to be ordered dealt with hermetic and magic.

I read the two I had bought and still could not explain the reason for the behavior of the gentleman.

A week later the phone call came that my third book had arrived. It was cloth bound in black with gold type. At least it looked valuable, after all the price was outrageous.

Once at home I got into the book. It dealt with a European mystic who gave detailed instruction for enlightenment.

The typeface of the book was awkward, the translation cumbersome and the subject matter boring. I regretted having spent the money and quit reading after the first chapter which dealt with the preparation to become a magician.

Somehow I had the feeling that I was being taken—I did not know how or why—but having spent the money on the books under the mysterious circumstances...weird to say the least.

I decided to forget the episode.

Little did I know then that it was not up to me to forget.

It was about 6 weeks after I had gotten the black book, when one day, out of the blue, the same gentlemen stood next to me in a computer store.

The last time I saw him was downtown. The first time I saw him was in the church in the east end and now we were in the suburbs in the west end of town.

"You are back from Austria", I said still surprised, "how was the trip."

He seemed to be in a hurry again and did not get into small talk. "You have to get past the first chapter, it is important for you. Just keep on reading, I am sure you will enjoy it."

He waved, he turned and left me standing astonished.

'Was I going mental?' I asked myself. This was getting to me. How did he know that I did not read past the first chapter of the book. How did he know were to find me? A very eerie feeling overcame me every time I thought of him.

For the next weeks I studied the book. It was still hard to read and awkwardly written, but I was determined to find out what this was all about.

I went through some of the exercises in the book—and lohen behold I experienced some very unusual things. I was sure that if I really wanted to, I could become a magician.

Did I want too?

Today the book is still on my shelf. Whenever I see it I say a quiet thank you to the gentleman with the bald head and the gold rimmed glasses.

Now, years later, the whole story appears unreal. Did this man really exist? I never met him again. Once I even looked for the second piece of paper he had given to me but I could not find it.

I was looking for some sort of stabilizer in this world, a piece of reality to proof to myself that I was not going out of my mind—or was I?

It was when I had that kind of a questioning mood that the calendar of the University fell into my hand. The course sticking out as if made for me was given by the philosophy department: "Existence and Reality".

Going through the course for one semester I was even more confused. What is reality? The chair I am sitting on, the body that has hands to type? My mind which thinks about the episodes in my past—whereby I still don't know where the mind is located?

One rainy afternoon I met a young man whom I had seen off and on in my work environment. He was a supplier to my company. He had some time to kill waiting for a purchase order and I was waiting for a taxi in the lobby.

I don't know how the discussion came to spiritualist mediums and mystics, but I know I described to this young man the gentlemen who gave me the book list. And wouldn't you know, this young man said "oh, I know him, he is from Austria and does a lot of good for young children. He raises money for a camp in the Alps."

At first I did not think we had the right person. But the more I heard about the escapades of this benefactor for children, I believed that it was the same man I had met.

I also learned, that the man lived in a little furnished room somewhere in the not so high class area and that he was just writing and meditating. Sometimes going for weeks without food.

That was hard to believe, but the young man told me that the Landlady had confided in him, that sometimes someone would come by and bring some food to the man and that person would not even know the man and just say 'I got the inspiration to come here with food'. Also there was no visible means of the man earning a living, but he would somehow get tickets to Austria and money would come to the children camp from Canada.

In retrospect I am glad that I had the encounter with the gentleman. I am glad that I read the book. I learned that there is still a lot to be learned about.

Thank you Sir, wherever you are. I am on my way.

# 18

## *Service around the stump.*

◆

### *First I was impressed, then I learned the truth: Don't trust a message in the dark.*

It was summer and the weekend promised to be full of sunshine—just the right weather to go for a drive. A friend called to invite me go to a Spiritualist Camp. I had read about those Camps and got all excited. After all, I envisioned floating trumpets, apparitions, tables to move through the air, voices from the other side...you know, all that scary stuff.

The place was located outside a small town, on a very picturesque lake. A cottage colony with an old hotel, a number of bed & breakfast places and private homes with shingles reading "healer", "psychic" "trance medium" and the like. There was also a church with a big bell and a hall for meetings and lectures.

After surveying the available accommodation we decided to drive to the highway and check into a Holiday Inn. Then we went back to sample the activities.

This weekend, a big name was expected to lecture on UFO's and messages from aliens. The assembly hall was packed.

The speaker had all the best credentials. A medical doctor, psychologist, author of numerous books...an authority on hallucinatory drugs, a family man—there was no doubt in my mind that I had finally found someone who would shed a light onto the psychic phenomena and maybe on his strange behavior.

I had met the speaker before while checking out the crystal skull and I was looking forward to getting more information on his watch.

A standing ovation greeted the guest speaker. He gave an excellent address. The facts were delivered with a dynamic that would have made a politician proud. Except, the facts were not exactly *academic* research but personal experiences with aliens, space ships and psychic phenomena.

The crowd was partial…the excitement in the hall could have been cut with a knife…the speaker worked the audience—every word was lapped up with fervor and enthusiasm.

There was no way for me to get close to the speaker after the lecture, however my friend knew him well and arranged for us to have a coffee with him, to have a private talk.

I must say, that I was impressed with the doctor's way of handling critical questions. He was a believer in his own story and there seemed to be no doubt in his mind that his experiences were factual, not hallucinations; that the messages from aliens of the 7th planetary reign (or something like it. I forgot the exact terminology) were meant for human consumption to warn them of upcoming encounters with the actual space people and to prepare the world for the kingdom to come, so to speak.

The man was real, intelligent and licensed to treat people. How could the message not be true?

Oh, by the way, he also told us of space babies and baby abductions by the aliens—very interesting.

The evening was spent visiting various psychics for messages and around midnight we attended a medium service at the stump. This was the remainder of an once majestic tree. Now the site of outdoor church services for spiritualists.

There was no light to speak of and the service was meant to be in the dark. The atmosphere was romantic more than ecclesiastical.

Some couples necked on the benches; discussion among the people; starlight and a sliver of the disappearing moon.

A medium started the service with a prayer. Then followed a poem or something like it. The real action came when the medium described a person in the audience. Remember it was dark and no one could see any further than five feet and only by walking around could I estimate the attendance to be around 70 people.

The description must have fitted one of the ladies, as she answered that the message was for her. Some relatives, long past over to the other side, were giving her advice on present family problems.

Another message was for a gentlemen not far from me and I tried to tune into his business affairs as the medium gave messages about his business partners. He was very quiet and did not answer to the medium other than acknowledging that he understood. The medium also told him of an illness he was grappling with and he got advice on what to do about it.

After the service I ambled up to the man and while it was hard to make out his face in the dark, I estimated him to be around 50, white and bald headed. He spoke with a southern accent as he answered my questions. Did the message make sense? Darn right it did. His business partner was cheating him and his kidney stones were painful.

I was impressed.

As I was fighting off the mosquitoes, which were bothering me all evening, I thought 'how could that lady have known about those facts'. There must be something to the mediums and I wanted to learn more.

We drove to the Holiday Inn determined to be back bright and early in the morning.

The hotel in the camp was in dire need of repairs. The windows had screens which needed fixing and the paint was only visible in spots and flakes.

I desired breakfast and then wanted to mingle with people.

The breakfast buffet proved clean and tasty. We shared our table with a group of young people who were here for the first time. They stayed at the hotel and shared a room. According to them "clean, not very comfortable but cheap".

From their stories I gathered that they were in a discussion group until the wee hours of the morning and did not get much sleep anyway. They too were critical observers and gave marks to the various mediums they had visited. Results so far 50:50.

The bald head struck my eye and I moved towards his table. Yes, he was the recipient of a message last night and yes he did talk to me afterwards.

He was very talkative now and told me that he was here to finally get his life together. He needed advice on his health and his business.

"If your partner is really cheating you and you are in financial trouble right now, why don't you call in the police to let them handle the case"? I asked.

"Well, I can't really prove that he is cheating. But business is really bad and he is not pulling his weight", was his answer.

I needed to get to the bottom of this and questioned him some more. He did not mind talking about himself, his life, his partner, his alcohol problem, his estranged wife and his children who did not want to see him.

Laying his life straight in front of a stranger I suddenly asked him "About that medium last night, did you ever meet her before or do you know who she is?"

"Oh yeah, I know her, she has been giving me good advice since yesterday afternoon. She is a good medium. After I told her about my business she gave me good counseling."

I now had second thoughts about midnight mediums.

# 19

## *Materializing a farm.*

◆

### *A couple believes that they created their new quarters with pictures on the fridge.*

My friend is a down to earth person. She has brought up her children in the good North American tradition. They are now married with children. She loves her grandchildren.

Something was missing in my friends life however, and she went on a spiritual quest. Churches, Cults, Gurus…nothing could hold her attention for very long.

One day she received a book from her brother about a new philosophical direction. She went for it.

Soon her bedroom walls were littered with little pictures. All representing something she would like to get out of life. There are some practical things, like a swimming pool, and some intangible concepts, like good health, friendship with spouse, clean environment….

Part of the teachings she is following declares the concept that you can create what you want. The principle that your mind creates your reality. And she truly believes that things she desires will materialize through her believes.

I have seen in my travels lots of people on their knees praying for one thing or another. I have read accounts of people who thought that they were in tune with God and could do no wrong—and read how they faltered, even died when thinking they could be like birds and tried to fly. Many people are as poor today as they were then. Prayer did not do it for a lot of them.

The pictures on the wall were things still in the future. How about the past? I needed to know. What better way than proving her wrong by finding little or big requests which had not materialized.

Well, I got my wish—she showed me a little box with drawings which used to decorate her bedroom and had been taken down. No, not because she changed her mind about getting this or that. And no, not because things took too long before they appeared. The reason they have come down is because the things she had focused on have actually become reality.

Thinking about this makes me shudder. Here is one of the little drawings in her box.

She and her husband were looking for a piece of property in the country side. A little farm, with commuting opportunities into the city to hold down a job.

They had searched and searched and could not find something that would fit into the allocated budget and provided all the amenities required for the couple.

One day they sat down and made a list of all the things which were required of the property. It covered the acreage, the price, the surroundings, the minimum size of the house, in short a dream was put on paper. It was then drawn into a picture and placed on the fridge with little magnets.

Every day the list came to the attention of the two. Since there were other important notes around it, like the things not to forget on the next shopping trip and future dentist appointments, the list with picture became part of the background furniture.

One day the two went on a trip to the west coast. Once the business part was finished a few days R & R followed. The mountains and the countryside was very impressive and just for kicks they inquired with real estate agents about available property and their prices in this area. They looked even at a few farms, which would in a way represent what they had been looking for in the East. Prices were lower here and the way of life seemed to be at a slower pace.

To make a long story short, one of the farms visited "felt good". A deal was struck with the owners and three days later the couple went back home, proud owners of property in the west.

They must have been in a daze because they never realized that someone had to move into the property and unless they considered moving west, who was going to live "in the middle of the boondocks "?

The day-to-day life took over immediately and shopping had to be done to restock the fridge. And there it was, their picture with the list of requirements for the future property. Hanging on the fridge door.

They looked at it then and to their amazement, all the little details they had dreamed of were incorporated in the newly acquired property. At the time of purchase they had not actually thought of the list to make check marks against each item. It had just "felt right". It was amazing how the new property exactly corresponded to their dream. However, the property was not near their present jobs. What to do.

It was decided to "take a chance on moving". And moving they did.

Today they are living in the "beautiful surroundings" among many buildings, which consist of barns, workshops and utility shelters, which my friend calls "Mytown", as clearly identified on the fridge list. The log home is there, so is the acreage—and the price was right too.

Coincidence?

Looking at the rest of the drawings in the box leads me to believe that maybe people do create their own reality. Materializing things may not be as impossible as it sounds.

# 20

## *Psychic fairs are "in".*

### *Just visiting is a great experience. The people seem to have a lot in common*

She was standing in front of the booth. A prospective customer for a book or a tape?

The booth attendant turned to her and asks if she could help.—She could.

Both ladies looked like in their thirties and they immediately got into a conversation about meditation music. A number of names came up, artists producing music which would induce an environment complimentary to the search for the higher self.

I walked over and introduced myself.

We are at a psychic fair held in one of those big hotels and the fair has been arranged like a trade show.

Booth spaces were bought by companies or individuals who cater to the philosophical search of the human being, the age old question "Why am I here on this Earth, where am I going—and do I come back?"

Looking at the sellers, many of them seem to have the right answer, judging by their sales literature.

Next to Psychic readers we find the manufacturer of all cotton clothing which is to promote a more natural living.

One booth sells handcrafted charms which will help to focus on the way to spiritual growth. The way may be walked with all leather sandals, imported from India, available next door.

Spiritual food is not forgotten, all natural, all healthy, all meant to help your body adjust to finer thought and to help in your search.

Exercisers will keep your body in shape, in case it is not and groups offering classes from exercising to meditation to love-ins to aura reading; from Taro interpretation to Rune reading...all is here at the fair.

Psychic readings can be booked immediately and seminars may be attended where the psychic phenomena is explained, demonstrated and interpreted through questions and answers.

It's a fair all right.

People come from far away to meet not only the sellers, but meet each other.

"My name is Ruth", said the sales lady.

I looked at her and she appeared to be a wholesome individual and if I had to guess I would put her living quarter on to a farm at the outskirt of the city. She was dressed in simple jeans skirt and blouse with a home made look about it. Her hair was simply combed back and held with a cotton bandanna, like a pony tail. Leather sandals complimented her looks. There seemed to be no make up, no perfume, no jewelry, all appeared to be natural material, including herself.

I looked towards the customer. She introduced herself as Margaret. There was something the two had in common. She too had no make up. Her hair was braided. She too looked like the new generation of seekers who abhor the technological advances of our time and would much rather go back to the horse and buggy era. Living off the land and not having to worry about air pollution. And without having to add a chemical laboratory to your body to sort out all the food additives in every meal of today.

Margaret held a tape in her hand and Ruth was playing the same in a demo machine at the table.

It must have been electronic music, sounding like the heavenly spheres had opened and were dowsing the world with peace.

I liked the tape and bought one.

Looking over the other books and tapes at the table I kept an ear on the conversation between Ruth and Margaret and all the other visitors walking by, sometimes buying, sometimes just saying hello.

It was a friendly atmosphere and it appeared that all who had in common the search for the higher self were more inclined to smile and to exchange an encouraging word.

I must have spent about a half an hour in the booth and received a cup of mint tea which was handed out by another seller of teas and herbs.

The books and tapes on display promised to help me. And they did. I felt calm inside just browsing.

I noticed Margaret later on in a booth of a card reader. I ambled by and waved but she was listening to the lady who had a regular deck of playing cards laid out in front of her and was gesticulating with her right hand which held a red handkerchief. I was wondering what kind of a symbol that was.

While this was not a medical exhibition, many of the groups and sales agents offered healing of some kind. Healing from ailments of the body. Some through laying on of hands, some through meditations, some through magnets and gadgets. They all seemed to be doing good business.

There were more books, more groups, more arts and crafts, more psychic readers—definitely an interesting group.

There was no lack of visitors either. Many paid the entrance fee to come and look and buy and grow.

A Saturday afternoon well spent.

I went home with my briefcase full of literature, names of psychics, groups and stores.

Was I a seeker?

# 21

## *Some healers have pull.*

◆

### *I was "slain in the spirit", but didn't believe it—*

A few spiritual healers were in town demonstrating their ability to heal instantly by laying on of hands. I was interested to see the anointed miracle worker, the Rev. White.

The church was in the north end of town and judging by the parking lot it was a sell-out performance. The entrance was crowded with people who wanted to get seated, ushers took them down the isle and made the congregation squeeze a bit together to find some more space on the benches, accommodating another person, another couple—me.

Organ music came through the loudspeakers—people were whispering. Still more ushers with more people. The church was packed and I estimated about eight hundred to a thousand people.

The couple on my right was about in their sixties; on my immediate left two females in their twenties. Throughout the church young and old, some children.

I am used to saying a prayer before sitting down, looking around, this did not to seem customary. People found a little spot and sat down, either looking ahead or flipping through papers, not too many seemed to know each other. "Very little interaction between the people", I thought.

Turning to my right I asked the man "Are you a member of the church"?

"No," he said," we are here for the first time, just to see the Reverend heal".

Same question to my left, similar answer.

Craning my neck I looked for the organ. There it was, right next to the speakers. A lady in her fifties was playing and another lady about the same age was sitting next to her. Supervising? Learning? I could not tell.

Two young men adjusted four microphones. Two mikes were attached to the pulpit and two stood on a platform.

The music went into a crescendo and then ebbed up and down into a low hum. The tunes were not familiar to me.

"Hi there, praise the Lord", a man about thirty years old was standing on the platform and holding one of the microphones.

"Let's praise the Lord together, altogether 'praise the Lord'".

Some of the congregation responded. Not good enough for him.

"We can do better than that, wake up, you are now under the spirit of the holy ghost, wake up. Again 'praise the Lord'".

This time it was better, obviously good enough for him. He said, "I am John, your host tonight. The Reverend White will be with you later on. He is meditating right now to enter in to the spirit of the Lord".

A long explanation came, regarding the healing about to be received by whoever was opening his heart to the Lord.

There were some disclaimers, that the Reverend White was not a healer but a man of God and that all healing was coming through the Holy Spirit. Reverend White was just a medium chosen by God to spread the message of Christ and to heal people like Jesus did—in the name of the Father.

They called a hymn and started singing. Not strongly supported by the congregation. A ladies choir brought some familiar tunes.

A prayer.

Some testimonies read out by John from letters received during the last week. People were healed from backaches, throat conditions; someone could see better and one person could walk again after having knee trouble for many years.

Every testimony was greeted with "praise the Lord" by John and upon directing the congregation everyone fell into "praise the Lord".

It was getting warm in the church. People took off jackets and my neighbor to the right opened his tie. I did the same.

Some more singing and then with big fanfares the Reverend White was announced.

Applause.

His voice was melodious and his opening statement was "Are you ready to receive the Lord today?"

The congregation was not responding vociferously enough. Upon prompting by the reverend the response "we are ready" droned through the church.

A sermon followed with Jesus the main character, Lazarus as an example and a promise that greater miracles would be seen once the master was gone.

The Lord's prayer in unison was followed by a hymn and then the Reverend White left the pulpit and grabbed one of the microphones including stand. His voice took on a low tone as he told his listeners that now the time had come for all of us to receive the Holy Spirit.

He then spoke fast, monotonous and without pausing to take a breath, at least that was what it felt like. His suggestion to us was to breathe in the spirit around us; to take the Holy Spirit into our hearts, to be overcome by spirit.

His voice was urging the congregation to close their eyes and to visualize the Holy Spirit enter.

Pointing to someone in the congregation he denounced the devil in the body of that person. People looked around, they did not exactly know who was meant.

Another direction: "A cancer in your body is trying to come to the forefront but in the name of the Lord I forbid the cancer to spread, I am asking in Jesus' name that you heal, heal, heal."

Again people craning their neck, to see to whom he was talking. If the person himself knew, well there was no recognition visible and the instruction was given that a lot of prayers were needed.

Three more were pointed at. A headache was taken away, a drinking problem solved and salvation given to some person not here in the church but sitting at home with a tumor.

So far not very impressive.

"Who is willing to receive Jesus right now?" the question was asked and the congregation was to raise their hand in the affirmative.

Many hands went up.

The reverend was praying for the people who had raised their hand and also for the ones that did not. All of us were to be saved by the Grace of God.

For the special healing ceremony people could step forward. White was going to practice laying on of hands, the formula described in the Bible.

His voice was urging the congregation to believe in the healing power of the Holy Spirit.

It was getting hotter in the church. White removed his jacket and worked with rolled up shirt sleeves.

Helpers appeared in front of the altar.

While White was still talking about the upcoming healing and laying on of hands he promised to walk through the aisles and touch everyone of us. He was about to bring miracles to everyone present.

He talked about faith. He talked about money. He talked about giving and receiving. The pinnacle was the dare to the congregation to show that they trusted in God with their material requirements as well as their health.

White wanted money. His group of helpers came through the aisles and collected in deep baskets, similar to the one I have under my desk for waste paper. There is no pun intended but the basket was full of bills—and not just $1.00 notes.

He sang a tune about Blessings from the Lord and the congregation was invited to join in the chorus.

It was getting warmer, some people were fanning themselves with magazines, brochures, pamphlets....

The reverend asked the troubled to come to the front to be healed. Behind him another group of helpers had taken their position with two ladies holding something that looked like a bunch of towels over their arms.

People walked to the front and lined up. White whispered something to each one and then with a loud "heal!" he would place his hand on the forehead of the person. The person seemed to fall backward and two male helpers caught them in their arms and slowly let them sink to the floor.

If it was a female who went down, the lady helpers with their towels would spread one over her legs and thighs.

After about four people on the floor, White explained that they were slain in the Holy Spirit.

There was excitement in the crowd as an elderly man in a wheel chair was pushed to the front and White announced that he should come to the forefront. The waiting crowd stepped aside. Some helpers lifted the gentlemen including his wheelchair onto the altar which now looked more like a stage.

In talking to the gentleman White held the microphone to him to let the congregation in on the conversation. The story was simple. The man could not work any longer in the warehouse were he was employed. His age he gave as 62. His medical condition was arthritis in the legs and his doctor had told him that he would be confined to the wheelchair for the rest of his life.

White went into a frenzy. He spoke about the devil having gotten hold of this body and trying to snatch it away from Jesus. He, White, was going to do the Lord's work in helping to return this man in to the fold of the followers of Jesus.

At the same time he was going to win over members in the congregation who were doubtful of the power of the Holy Spirit.

The Reverend spoke fast and convincingly. He pleaded with Jesus to give him the strength to heal this man.

Then he went behind the wheelchair and still keeping his microphone open, that the audience could partake in the short prayer, White put his right hand onto the forehead of the man and shouted "heal, heal, heal". With that the man seemed to slump in his wheel chair.

The congregation was on their feet. They wanted to see exactly what was going on up front and stood in the aisles and on the benches. It was hard to get a good look at the stage.

Reverend White turned his attention to the waiting line up. More prayers, more slayings...now, it went in a rapid progression. The floor was filled with bodies.

When one of the bodies on the floor stirred, the helpers were right there to give the person a hand to get up and leave the stage.

"All you people, please sit down. You are witnessing the power of the Holy Spirit and I will come to you as well." White urged the congregation. He then invited more to come to the front for a healing, as the line up was getting down.

I decided to go to the front.

There is nothing wrong with me. I am healthy. The experience of being "slain in the spirit", however, was something I wanted to learn.

Once on the stage, I could look at some of the bodies. Not all of them were "out", as I had thought. There must have been at least 10—15 men and women who were just lying there, with their eyes open, but not stirring. I was surprised. Did they needed a rest?

Three more to go before my turn came around.

The lady "in treatment" right now was trying to tell the Reverend about her ailments, but he was not listening. He talked into the microphone about the tremendous power on the platform and how the spirit will take care of things.

A touch on the forehead and two men slowly let the lady sink to the floor. There she lay like dead. A helping church worker placed a towel over her skirt and legs.

Two more to go.

The young man speaking to White now was stuttering. He wanted his help to get rid of the affliction. White did nod his head and touched the temple of the man. Two helpers slid him to the floor.

I took a good look at the young man and checked what he was wearing. I was going to try to speak to him afterward. This was a good candidate for me to check on the Reverend's score card.

One more to go, a gentleman in his fifties I would say, quite well dressed in a business suit. He had not even loosened his tie even though it was very hot on the stage.

Only now did I notice a couple of video cameras on the side lines. Spot- and floodlights made it even hotter up front.

The second lady next to the Piano was actually manipulating the control buttons for the microphones. There was also a light man who stood very close to the cameraman.

White interrupted the line by paying attention to the wheelchair person. The man had been quite awake and looking around for some time.

"How are you feeling", White asked.

"Fine", was the answer.

"What is your first name?"

"Hugo".

White raised his voice into a staccato and told the audience that God had just told him that this man was an example to the congregation. He spoke to Hugo.

"God made you whole. The Holy Spirit has touched you. You are now able to walk again. Get up and leave your wheelchair—in the name of Jesus Christ".

Suddenly the church was quiet. A pin drop would have sounded like an explosion.

All eyes were focused on Hugo. People started to stand up again in the aisles and on the pews.

Hugo seemed to hesitate. Then with the help of Reverend White he got up and stood in front of the altar.

Applause from the congregation.

White took Hugo's arm and slowly walked with him along the front of the rostrum.

The applause grew and the organist intoned "How great Thou art."

White took Hugo to a seat towards the back of the church. While he was walking through the aisles hands were stretched towards him and he took them, touched some on their foreheads and while Hugo walked slowly, he nevertheless smilingly made his way half way up the church. When he sat down, the audience applauded again, while still singing.

I had the best view in the house from my elevated position at the altar. All of this happened right in front of my eyes. I saw the smile on Hugo's face. I noticed the doubting look when he was asked to stand up—it looked like I had just witnessed a miracle.

Another song and then White came back to look after us. It was my turn. He whispered to me "I know through God that you have a secret disorder and I am authorized to heal you in the name of the Lord".

With that he touched my head and I felt a push back. At the same time two men grabbed me from the back and I was pulled to the floor.

The whole thing happened so quickly, that I did not struggle, because I was so perplexed. I just let it happen.

Once on the floor, I looked up to see what was going on, but just as I had seen from the back seat, the show went on.

I moved to get up and immediately a helper was there to give me a hand. With a "God bless you brother", they led me to the stairs to go back to the aisle and return to my seat.

I was still in shock.

There was no power of the Holy Spirit to push me back, it was the hand and arm of White. With the first movement to the back the two helpers behind me did the rest to get me to the ground.

This was a scam. How could it have been so blatant and not recognized?

I had to look for a while before I found my pew. One of the young ladies who sat next to me touched me as I was going by.

"That was beautiful, the way you were touched by God", she said. "I was watching and saw a great blue light all around you, even when you lay on the floor".

"Thank you", I mumbled.

Here I was convinced that I had just witnessed the biggest fraud there was—and this young lady had seen something I was not aware of. Was she imagining things?

I sat down. The gentlemen to my right leant over to me and whispered "My wife saw a great white light standing next to you at the altar."

Looking at her she nodded in my direction and he continued "she knows what she is talking about. She has been a seer since she was a little child. She thinks good vibrations are all around you and you are a lucky person". With that he leaned back and watched the goings on in front.

A Psychiatrist could have declared me ready for the loony bin. What was this? Blue light, white light? My foot—there was no light, there was no spirit—it was White who pushed me back and it were his accomplices who pulled further and let me sink to the ground.

I watched more closely, as White was still laying his hand on the foreheads of people. They were still popping like flies. The empty wheelchair up front stood there as a reminder that God worked miracles here—or was it the Devil?

Until the end of the service, I did not really pay much attention to the front anymore. I looked around. Tried to find some happy people who had just received a miracle and I found some. People would smile keep their eyes closed and seemed to live in bliss. Others were crying—for pain or joy—I could not tell.

When it was all over, I wanted desperately to talk to two persons: the stutterer and Hugo the wheelchair man.

As if by another miracle, both of them did not come out of the church. I was one of the first ones out and stood at the door eying all who emerged from the wide open door. Those two were not among them.

When the outflow had turned to only the odd person coming out, either limping or supported by people to the right and left of them, I went back inside.

The helpers were dismounting the cameras and the microphones. White was standing in front talking to the pianist. They seemed to be in an argument.

Neither of the two expected persons were here. That was strange.

I walked up to the front and ambled over to White. He stopped his shouting at the lady and faced me. "What can I do for you?"

He said the two must have gone already, he had not kept an eye on them. The wheelchair was still standing up front.

Then I was dismissed with the excuse that the church had to be cleaned and everyone had to leave.

I was very suspicious.

Call it co-incidence, call it fate. It was about four months later that I was walking through a shopping plaza and before me walked a young man who looked familiar. I stepped up and touched his arm. Yes, as he looked at me I recognized the stutterer.

"May I ask you a personal question", I started politely. He looked surprised.

There was no sign of recognition on his face that he remembered me. That I did not expect anyway.

In very clear pronunciation he ask, "what can I do for you?" I told him that I thought that I knew him from the healing service in the church and just wanted confirmation that he really was the person I thought he was.

Was it my imagination or did he really blush? He then almost stuttered as he said "Yes, that was me".

"Did you get a healing from Reverend White?"

"Yes I did—and I am very grateful. Good afternoon."

With that he turned around and walked on.

# 22

# *The menu includes Soya Burgers.*

◆

***Watch the health food scene exploding. I will want the taste to come with it—***

The store was at a highway intersection about 60 miles from the city core. It smelled good when I walked in, 'incense burning' I thought.

All items I could see were handmade.

Ceramic, leather, wood, cotton, wool—those seemed to be the materials used most in all the wonderful things on display.Dolls for children of all ages, clothing for summer and winter, kitchen items, gifts, handmade cards for all occasions, soapstone carvings, paintings, photographs—it was a pleasure to walk through the store and admire the ingenuity of people to create all these wonderful things.

The prices seemed quite a bit higher than those in department stores, but then this stuff was hand made. Created with love.

A little tea sampling room added to the charm of the store and the customers enjoyed the whole environment obviously, listening to the comments of the patrons who looked at, touched and cuddled many of the items on display.

Folders of self help groups were laying on the counter, magazines touting the age of Aquarius and the holistic generation.... It appeared that there were enough people out there somewhere to care for other human beings, to effect a change in thinking patterns for a better world.

I talked to the young man operating the cash register, a gadget which would bring one back to reality after letting the thoughts fly into the heavens, and he appeared older and wiser with his beard and pony-tail. He was friendly and helpful. Apparently at peace with himself, or well trained in the art of salesmanship. People bought, despite the high price.

The brochure in the rack advertised a restaurant in the city. It touted the best natural foods anywhere. I took a copy and asked the bearded friend about his opinion.

"Have a Hamburger there, it's the best in the world".

Somehow the remark troubled me as I left the store to drive back to the city. I did not quite know what it was, but there was a food store and a restaurant serving the best natural foods—and I wanted to taste them.

I changed my mind quickly after arriving.

There was a variety of meals available, all vegetarian. Probably all good for someone who enjoys that kind of fare. I was looking for the hamburger and somehow was still wondering about the bearded clerk who would fit right into this environment as all male patrons seemed to be bearded and a lot of pony tails with rubber bands showed the fashion trend. Ladies had obviously a liking for straight hair, simply combed back and held back by old fashion combs.

The hamburger was on my mind. I asked the waiter. He pointed to the menu and then it all fell into place. No meat but soya and other meat substitutes high in protein, low in fat—the hamburger of the new generation.

I decided on a chamomile tea and some whole wheat bread with honey. This was the closest I could come to my normal eating habits and I wasn't ready yet, if ever, to change them.

Afterwards I looked at the many items in the store. I was amazed to see that old fashion bulk buying had returned to North America. The beans and peas, the flower and the candies, all in big containers with a little shovel to help yourself filling the required amount into brown bags.

There must be a market for this stuff because brand labels had already developed with guaranteed natural ingredients. Move over General Foods and beware of the new breed shopper. Unless of course the large food processing plants were already in control of the "new brands" and just found a market niche to develop.

Was I out of step with the world? Did time bypass me when I worked at least eight hours a day to accumulate some riches for future security and present pleasure?

I decided to keep an eye on the trends in the food world to see how they related to the spiritual quest and the peace movement. There seemed to be thoughts and actions in common with those groups.

# 23

## *Healing like Jesus.*

***Some people claim to have a direct line and work with the teacher of 2000 years ago. They say he is around to lend a helping hand, so to speak—***

His business card announces him as a spiritual healer. Born in France, he has a good command of the English language with a charming French accent. He counsels and is even called overseas to help someone in need.

I know of one lady who sends him plane tickets to different parts of the world, if she is in need of healing.

The clientele comes by recommendation. Jean is not advertising but he seems to be busy with appointments.

He claims that his healing power comes from the highest source: Jesus. A local TV station once interviewed him and one of his clients. It appears from the account of the witness (I watched the video tape), that real miraculous healing took place.

Jean just shrugs," what do you expect—read the Bible, it's all there. Jesus is still working today and uses my hands and other people's of course."

Wanda, a friend of his, is living nearby she too is channeling Jesus. In meditation she is receiving messages for her clientele. Advice on spiritual matters, daily living concerns or answers to any questions one might have.

Her Bed & Breakfast Mansion is used for spiritual retreats, teaching meditation and other esoteric practices. According to one regular visitor: 'the vibration is absolutely great'.

Both, Jean and Wanda, have their spiritual guide Jesus in common. But with further analysis, these two also have in common a desire to help other people.

I have met at least 9 persons who had contact with either Wanda or Jean, and all are absolutely convinced that the power of Jesus is within them.

The sincerity of the practitioners beliefs and the fervor with which they defend the message of Christ may just give them an edge over "orthodox" preachers and healers.

Wanda charges for her services—sometimes. Jean does not take any money. He will accept travel expenses if he has to go out of town.

# 24

## *Cruising under the stars.*

### *Another vacation, another experience with Astrology—*

The cruise was just a Caribbean cruise. Not one of the specially advertised "Psychic Cruises" were a Psychic is on board and gives readings to the passengers. No, just a regular cruise.

It was therefore just out of the blue that the cruise director announced that we would get an astrologer on board in the next port. She was going to give lectures in introductory astrology. Anyone interested was invited to go to the gambling hall in the morning after breakfast to learn about the mysterious powers of the stars.

I was not alone on this cruise and a quick discussion with my partner and a bunch of friends brought us all into the lecture.

The lady teaching the course was interesting. She made the subject matter fun and still brought out good information when she used examples of real life people.

She went through the calendar and volunteers of each star sign stood up and were read. Most of them agreed, that what the astrologer had told them applied to them.

She went into past, present and future and while explaining the houses and interacting stars and planets she was looking for a Sagittarius to volunteer.

A stab from my partner and my hand went up. I was on stage. The usual routine about date of birth and place of birth and then a couple of remarks, which I thought of as platitudes, anybody could have guessed them just by looking at me. As I said, those were my thoughts.

Then after looking at the black board again where she had drawn a horoscope, she turned to me and said "You have just very recently married…." she said some more about me, but it just did not register anymore. I don't remember even that I blushed.

Oh my friends gave it to me afterwards. This eternal skeptic got it with both barrels.

What happen?

Well, for many years I thought of myself as a bachelor and successfully kept that marital status as 'single' (after a divorce). There were ample opportunities in my life to re-marry again or to take on a permanent relationship, but I did not have the inclination.

I married very early in my life and after the first 4 years my wife and I decided that married life was not for us. Now, 25 years later this astrologer tells me that I got married again—very recently.

She was absolutely right.

Just before the cruise I had decided to let my girlfriend move into my house with me. This was a big decision on my part, as it constituted a commitment just as good as marriage. The astrologer picked that out of my horoscope. That got me worried.

Is our life preordained? Is anything we do already engraved in the stars? Do we actually decide things or is all decided already ahead of time?

And our birthday, what could it possible have to do with our action in later life? Did a greater force decide what date and in what place we are to be born?

Questions over questions.

Every time on of those psychics, astronomers or whatever else they call themselves hit into the right notch, I become concerned.

Why don't we teach those things in school? If everyone were taught astrology and we all could play with the date provided in the stars, maybe our science would change, maybe our religion would change—maybe the world would change—after all, big brother may be watching.

This cruise was an enjoyable one. I wanted to forget the astrologer but my friends reminded me that my life had been like an open book when I was on the stage.

My little secrets should be my own, I don't want the public to participate in my life—but of course I did volunteer. No one else is to blame but me. But then I did not expect the astrologer to be so dead on.

# 25

## *Sitting in the "Lotus Position".*

### *Twist your body into pain, overcome the pain...and bingo, enlightenment is on it's way.*

It was a sunny Sunday morning and as many people were going to Church, I felt right at home with the crowd streaming towards the doors of a huge cathedral. There a welcoming committee stood to greet all comers. However, just before reaching the sweeping staircase I turned right. I knew I had to use the side entrance.

Once there, a crudely made sign pointed to stairs leading into the basement.

I followed a few more arrows and felt I was roaming the catacombs of Rome. The Church must have been at least 150 years old, the stones were rough cut and a musty smell lingered in the halls I was walking through.

It was amazing how quiet it was down here. Not a sound of the many people upstairs in the church. Not a sound around me indicating that other people occupied the basement. But I knew better.

At the end of the corridor a heavy curtain reached from the ceiling right down to the floor. It was parted in the middle to show an entrance into a room, dimly lit. I walked in. My objective was reached.

Three weeks earlier I had noticed a little advertisement for a beginner's meditation class. A society was welcoming new members. The name of the group sounded Indian or Hindu and I wanted to know more.

The first day a bearded master greeted me with a handshake that never seemed to end. His smile made his mouth appear to reach from ear to ear, literally, and his voice reminded me of a deep drum-like monotone.

I took notice of about 10 other people who were sitting on their crossed legs and eyes closed, just sitting, hands on their knees, palms up.

I was given instructions by the master to just follow the others in their seating arrangement and he gave me a little pillow "for newcomers". I squatted down to, what I later learned, was the lotus position. My eyes closed I waited, but I could not help but squint from time to time just to see if anything around me had changed. Nothing had changed, except the group had grown to about 25.

The carpet on the floor muffled all walking sounds and only from time to time the sound of the master could be heard. If the position I was sitting in would not have been so awkward I would have fallen asleep.

Time was going by and at one of my sweeping squints I looked at my watch. A half an hour had passed and nothing happened. I was wondering if my $5.00 per session voluntary donation, twice a week, was teaching me patience or meditation.

Finally, the master could be heard from the front of the room. In his monotone deep sounding voice he asked us to keep our eyes closed. He started to read chapters from the Upanishads, which are part of Vedic literature and considered the basis of many of the Eastern religious philosophies, specifically Buddhism.

We learned something about the process of creation and the nature of the soul.

My feet were killing me. My legs were tingling with the typical sign of circulation problems. My mind was interested, my body was bored stiff, so to speak.

We learned to hum a Mantra and sit again quietly for a while and after about two hours, I could hardly walk or stand. I had to support myself on the wall to keep my feet from giving in.

The master noticed my problem and gave me good advice on how to overcome the struggle between body and mind by regularly exercising the lotus position until one day my mind would be free from the burden of the flesh and I could soar free through the Universe.

This now was my fourth try to shed my body from my mind. Many of the group had assembled already. Everyone awaiting the master in lotus position, palms up, eyes closed.

It had become much easier for me to sit in this strange way and I must say, that once the body got used to it, it was very comfortable. Two weeks of muscle ache were forgotten by now.

The yogi arrived to again read from the book. Wisdom, claimed to be assembled 1000 years before the birth of Christianity, was given to us. We learned about the various forms and bodies our souls have to go through before reaching our final form. This was the explanation of reincarnation. I listened carefully.

A mantra again, quiet contemplation, discussion...a Sunday morning differently arranged than upstairs in the church but definitely concerning similar goals: Find out more about our life on earth, why are we here, why are we born and what is beyond and who and where is God?

I was surprised that churches would lend cellar rooms to other religious organizations. In this case, the group was not necessarily competing with the church, but in medieval times every participant would have been burnt on the stake. The master was teaching pagan doctrines, not Christian philosophy—I could see myself in front of the Inquisition....

A few enquiries to church administrators and I knew about the modern generosity of some Christian groups. They will lend their basements to charities or other non-profit organizations to share the burden of overhead.

After about 6 weeks of attending meditation class I felt that I became quite adept in turning my mind off my bodily functions and with daily exercises I was able to meditate quite easily.

Did I float through the Universe? Well, not exactly but something left my body at times. Where did it go? Maybe just hover over my body to look from the outside at this bundle of flesh sitting in a strange position.

It was the same experience I had when sitting in an easy chair listening to a special tape on goal setting with a guided meditation. This method did not require going through bodily exercises in order to clear the mind. But who knows which is the right way.

I kept on reading more about Eastern philosophy but abandoned the lotus position. Somehow I felt our culture in general, and I specifically, was not ready to take on the foreign teachings.

# 26

## *The Yogi Guru is into politics.*

◆

### *He may be able to advise statesmen, but he could not get it together with me. Am I Irish?*

The display ad read something like 'you are lucky that I am coming into your town because I am busy in the capital to advise the leaders of our country'.

Well, the psychic advertising his ability, guaranteed over 90% accuracy. His credentials were, among others, that he was written up in many national and international newspapers and journals. I could not wait to meet him.

The appointment was made through his secretary. Luckily within ten days there was a spot. To be sure, $75.00 had to be paid before the session began.

My disappointment came when I met the Yogi. Rather than being from India, something one could expect from his name, he was of European decent and looked not anything like a psychic—whatever that means.

I felt strange that this man was in town only temporarily but had a business setup, which indicated permanency. However, I was not to judge the surroundings, I was in search of the psychic—the real thing.

An old fashioned tape recorder was set up on the desk and a pad in front of the Yogi contained a number of doodles. A pen nearby completed the assembly of working tools. I was motioned to sit in front of the desk. The tape recorder was rolling.

After a number of minutes, a phone call, which he answered and a knock on the door, which he attended to, the master finally turned his attention to me and asked me a number of personal questions. I told him that I was a journalist and that I wanted to meet a real psychic. I wanted proof.

After another interruption, the Yogi turned to me "I am really sorry, but today is a bad day for me, the political situation is very strenuous and all my psychic power is directed towards saving this country and advising our politicians on the future of our economical and political difficulties. If you don't mind please let me return your money."

I was not about to give up that easily. "Don't worry about your time right now, I will come back some other day. I will phone your office and will make another appointment if that is o.k. with you."

It was.

When the next appointment came around I was surprised to learn that the Guru was not in the office, but I was referred to an Astrologer in the office next door. That of course was not in my plan and I insisted on waiting for the Yogi to return.

After about one hour of waiting in the office, with only a short break for a coffee and a donut, the master arrived. In his entourage was a Public Relations person (which I happen to recognize) and while walking into his office they were discussing publicity in newspapers and magazines. I was ignored.

After a short while I knocked on the door and introduced myself as having the appointment. The Yogi wanted to weasel out. He tried once more to suggest the Astrologer. My disapproval was firm. He tried to offer the money back once more—no deal. Finally he asked me to wait another 20 minutes and I would have my consultation. I agreed.

Ten minutes later I was invited into his office. The same setting as before.

With eyes closed the master was talking about the political situation of the country. Today's headlines in the newspapers were the topics. Predictions were made which in retrospect did not materialize.

I interrupted: "I am more concerned with my personal affairs. I would appreciate a demonstration of ESP, which I can relate to. I want to be convinced that it exists."

It appeared that I had the Guru's attention, he was listening to me now and I kept on talking.

"There are many psychics around who take people's money but do not perform and therefore I have come here to meet the real McCoy. Also, I read that some of the psychic streams of information, if they really do exists, come in waves which the medium cannot control…"

He now interrupted me: "I can control the psychic information to 99%. I do about 1000 consultations a year and offer the refund guarantee if people are not satisfied. Only two people requested their money back so far."

After a little pause he continued "You are not born in this country, I feel that your parents came from Europe, maybe from England".

That was shocking news. For one my accent cannot hide my heritage and with my name—I can hardly claim that it is Irish. Even a non-psychic would have done better.

"No, I, my parents and my grandparents were born in Germany", I answered.

"Aah yeah, were they in the agrarian field?"

"No"

"Tradesman?"

"No".

"What was your Grandfather's name?"

"One of them was named August"

"Hm. I am just doodling around."

After a pause "I am frightfully sorry, but I find it impossible to hit your wavelength. I am floating around and I am turning out something completely mediocre—and I don't want to do that. Might that be that on account of projections or because of the difficulty I have run into because of my political predictions. I just cannot establish a flow with you.

"Let me make a suggestion. Simply send me one of your friends or acquaintances. They will have a consultation and then you can study the tape and judge for yourself. You can then assess the validity. It just happens every 100 or 150 times that I can not establish the flow, the psychic connection.

"Whether the problem is with you or with me I cannot ascertain at the moment, but I am under severe pressure on account of politics…."

The session broke up. It was just a waste of his and my time.

Is he a Guru? Is he a master, a Psychic?

While mentioning the story to some friends one told me that she heard from a friend that he was "really right on".

Well, you never know for sure.

# 27

## *The circle.*

◆

***I joined the circle to get some good information. I took them with a grain of salt.***

I heard of the "Circle" from one of the visitors to the Psychic Fair. Was I invited? Well, she had to ask.

Soon my phone rang and the invitation was there. "Next Friday evening at Jerry's house". The address followed.

Friday did not come a day to soon, as I was anxious to find out how the Circle worked. Apparently all kinds of wondrous things had happened to the sitting members. My open mind coupled with curiosity and a healthy amount of skepticism should bring me closer to the events of the paranormal, if there was such thing.

Jerry's house was in the suburbs. Parking was a problem, as there were already 4 cars in his driveway and the street in front of the house had a line up covering the fronts of 5 more houses. All of those people are at Jerry's, I wondered?

The door was open. I knocked anyway and then stepped in, as there was no reply. I heard from the rooms to the left the chatter of people and ventured into the house.

It was the living room and about 15 people made themselves comfortable on chairs, sofas and the carpeted floor. I was greeted as the 'Newcomer' and invited to join the group with a cushion on the floor.

Someone closed the door and turned on a tape recorder. Music flowed through the room and the talk broke up. A man sitting on one of the chairs next to the stereo unit began to speak. He invoked the eternal spirit to join us in our quest for higher knowledge. After he finished the group intoned "Ooooooouuuuummmmmm"

Now came the official greeting. I was pointed out as the new member of the group. "Welcome" was murmured by the group. Then one by one each said "My name is…." Everyone introduced themselves to me with their first name. I was asked to say my name and what my reason for coming here was.

This was a tricky question to answer. If the group was into mind reading, they would know that I was curious. They would also know that I had been making my rounds to groups like this to search for the truth in their work. From experience I knew that people like me, who do not become believers the first evening are treated as skeptics and are not really welcomed. We "interrupt the energy flow" among the others, who wholeheartedly agree with everything said and going on.

"I am a searcher for the eternal truth", I said. This was not a lie and a big enough statement to hopefully satisfy their expectations. It did.

It was Jerry who was in command. He had the controls of the stereo next to him and the music, a slow beat, relaxing sound, was turned up after I spoke.

We started a breathing exercise. Jerry counted aloud. Inhaling was up to the count of 8, then we had to hold the breath for 4 counts and exhale slowly to the count of ten. This went on for a while and Jerry asked us to keep the rhythm of breathing while he gave a guided meditation. Our minds were to follow him over the hills and dales of the countryside.

There were suggestions of colorful pictures and nearly at the end there was a concentration on one's own body to strengthen all organs and to heal whatever needed healing. Then came a long pause for individual meditation.

The music kept on playing easy sounds. Only the sound of breathing could be heard over the music.

Suddenly one of the group spoke out.

I opened my eyes and looked around.

Everyone else still had his or her eyes closed. Jerry seemed to have his chin on his chest. His arms were stretched out as if to receive something from heaven.

It was Joanna who, with her face looking to the ceiling, spoke to someone unseen—at least by me. She said "yes" and "no" and seemed to be taking some instructions.

The rest of the group did not seem to be disturbed by the one way conversation.

Next to me Henry was mumbling something and I looked over to my right.

Henry was slumped over and spoke undiscernibly to himself.

All others eyes were closed.

I moved my body slightly to get closer to Henry. I wanted to know what he was talking about.

While I was successful in hearing him, I still could not understand what he was saying. It sounded gibberish to me.

The beat of the music picked up.

There were smiles on some of the faces in the group and even though Jerry had somehow managed to get the light down next to nothing, the faces could be distinguished and everyone seemed to be either happy or sleeping.

Jerry stirred. His hands moved closer to his body as if to hold a treasure close to him.

Others moved—I quickly closed my eyes. I did not want them to catch me watching.

I heard some of the group members taking a deep breath and the sound of stretching after a good nights rest came from across from me. My eyes opened slightly. I squinted and noticed that some of the group were sitting quietly with their eyes open.

I too opened my eyes and sat quietly.

From the stereo came the hum of a familiar church tune. The group members fell into the hum and it appeared that everyone was happy and well.

Once the tune ended, the stereo made the click, telling us that the tape had stopped.

Jerry started to speak and looking in my direction he asked whether I was O.K..

I told him that I was.

"How do you feel", he wanted to know.

"Comfortable, peaceful inside", I answered.

He nodded. "Any unusual experience during the meditation?"

I shook my head "Nothing unusual".

Jerry's look went to Henry who had a big smile on his face.

"Tell us about your meditation experience. Where did you go? What did you do?"

Henry took the ball. He explained that after the guided meditation he went on his own. Apparently he was asking his spiritual guide to show him the Akashik Records.

Jerry got all excited as Henry spoke now.

"I was taken to a big hall and I could see scrolls and scrolls. There were books and records, drawers full of things and I was led to a particular section of the room and it looked like the personal records of each person on earth were here."

Henry went on to say that he did not really "see" those records, but that inside himself he just "knew" what it was. His guide then gave him a crystal and "I was astonished that the crystal piece in my hand contained information which I could understand. I just looked at it and my guide asked me to read aloud the information.

"It was truly amazing. Here was a story about another planet where somehow a person like myself and some of my friends were planning a voyage to some distant star. The story was like a document engraved into the crystal. Absolutely amazing. Even my wife played part in that story…and Jerry, you too were part of the crew…amazing, amazing".

Henry was obviously astonished about his experience.

The group listened intently. Some shrieks accompanied his story from time to time. It was Judy who showed her enthusiasm. Later I learned that Judy was Henry's wife.

Jerry told Henry that he had really taken a good "trip" and that he should meditate some more on the information he had received.

"There is a message in that message" he emphasized. "Something you can use at the present time. Look for it".

Jerry questioned everyone, one by one in the circle.

A number of people saw colors, like rainbows coming into their body. One was riding the clouds with a large piano, playing the most beautiful concerto.

"Is the piano meaningful to you?, Jerry questioned.

"Yes, it sure is. I want one and learn how to play."

"Then your piano is on the way!". With that Jerry turned to the next person.

Joanna gave a report of her experience. She had seen her recently departed mother and had received some instructions from her. Apparently the estate was not quite settled and there was something her mother wanted to have given to someone else. Also she talked about a hidden treasure of family jewellery and stamps which she wanted Joanna to have.

I was getting itchy. Here seemed to be some proof of survival after death—if Joanna could come up with the hidden treasures.

Jerry interrupted my thoughts by telling Joanna "Do not speak to anyone about this. Just follow the instructions of your mother and execute her last will. Everyone here in the group will respect your privacy in the matter. Do follow spirit's advice".I had some choice thoughts for Jerry and his advice. Suddenly Jerry looked over to me and tried to make contact with my eyes. I closed them. Somehow I was ashamed of my thoughts—and somehow Jerry seemed to know.

After everyone had reported, the group stood up, held hands and sang a song about happiness and peace. I felt they were singing it for me, as everyone looked at me as if to say "Welcome to the Circle".

There were apples, bananas and cookies in the kitchen and everyone mingled and chatted. It was comfortable but I had a hard time keeping myself away from Joanna. I knew that I would be asking questions if I would get into a conversation with her.

A note in my diary will remind me to check maybe after a year or so to see if I can get to the bottom of it.

# 28

## *What is in the cards for me?*

### *A look at the Tarot. Is there a secret force shuffling? Can the cards predict the future?*

The seminar was advertised in the window of the bookshop. It was the countries foremost expert in the Tarot who had already 5 books published on the subject—and he was going to tell all. Especially to beginners.

Who could resist the temptation?

The Rotunda of the library was packed. Mostly females, maybe 200 of them. Even the TV cameras were there with the bright lights disturbing some of the visitors who asked them to be pointed in a different direction.

Our speaker was introduced by the bookstore manager. He pointed out that the author had come a long way and that his books were available at his location. Matter of fact, a public "reading" demonstration was planned for the lunch hour crowd tomorrow, right in the shop, no charge.

Applause. Then our visiting expert took the microphone.

He was around 40 or 45 and was dressed in casual attire. His demeanor displayed confidence as he explained the history of playing cards. The reference to monks of the $14^{th}$ century; the speculations about the name Tarot; the various expressions used by artists to depict the faces of the cards; Allister Crawley's connection to a new deck—it was an interesting story, told in an interesting and well modulated way. Our speaker had the group well in his hand. It was quiet and you could have heard a pin drop.

The various pictures of the cards were explained. What do they mean when they are placed in a certain position of the game layout? Who controls the cards? How could they foretell the future? Was it black magic?

For two hours the listeners were spell bound, so to speak. A demonstration with a volunteer showed how it was done. References to his introductory books and his manuals were interspersed with comments of his past studies on the subject. He established himself as the authority.

The volunteer had the cards read. To the question "Do you understand the situation?" she just nodded.

A short break gave us the opportunity to browse through the book shelves set up by the store. Only our speakers' books were on display. Many were bought.

"Who would like to take a full course in the interpretation of the cards?"

The list was there for people to pre-register. About 50 names and addresses appeared before the break was over.

Can the Tarot predict the future? Will we accept the fact that the card showing the "Hermit" explains a loneliness around us in a personal relationship? It could mean also that a certain wisdom is being achieved. Particularly if the card appears in position 5 of the layout "The Way"—it will show that the person for whom the cards are read should display trust and confidence. There should be a certain amount of inner searching of the way ahead which maybe achieved with fasting, meditation and listening to the inner voice to give direction.

Should the card appear in position 3 in the same layout for you, it could mean that you are holding back and that you are contemplating your loneliness, which you could enjoy, or which could mean that you are doubting yourself and you could suffer from being alone.

We were shown a number of different layouts in use by Tarot card readers. The simple cross is played with 4 out of the deck of 78 cards. Card number one on the left side is to convey the subject matter. The second card, on the right will show a solution to the problem, should however not be considered, as it is the wrong solution. Only card 3 at the top of the cross shows the right way which should be taken to achieve the goal which will appear in the form of card 4 at the bottom of the layout.

More volunteers were requested from the audience. They asked a quiet question and then pulled out some cards which the reader was placing on a flip chart, for all to see. Oversized cards were then shown to the listeners to explain what the meaning of the particular cards in relation to their position was.

At the end of each reading the question was asked "Do you understand?" No one complaint. No one did not understand.

I was very curious. My investment in his handbook and a set of cards was considerable, as I was not about to become a professional card reader and charge people for the reading to get my money back. Even though I see the advertisements all the time and figure that it must be a profitable business.

The first opportunity saw me relaxing at home with the cards spread out in front of me. Face down, as requested in the book. Then I thought of a question to a current problem. I gave Infinite Intelligence some time to arrange the cards for a correct answer and then I pulled the cards out of the deck and arranged them in the layout of the cross.

My first card was the Ace of Cups. This was explained as the lucky card. It was dead on with my thoughts of winning in the lottery. The Ace was supposed to tell me I have all the chances inside of me and that I am on the right track in my life.

Card number two was the 8 of clubs. This apparently is the card showing that "something is brewing". The time is right and something is on the way.

At the top of the cross was the 3 of clubs. A mile stone was achieved. I was at the top and looking down at all the tribulations of the past.

From the way the picture of the 3 of cubs appears, a celebration is in the offing. 3 maidens are happy and in a festive mood. That was also the explanation in the book. Something has been received.

Did the Tarot know?

I was about to find out.

Three days later I checked my lottery tickets and I won some money.

Coincidence?

# 29

## *Back to meditation—a guided one.*

*How meditation can bring extra ordinary experiences and knowledge. A story about my toe and a lady with a house.*

It looked like a store with the curtains drawn in front of the merchandise. A sign advertised it as a spiritualist church. Today was Tuesday, meditation night.

The inside of the "store" was decorated in what appeared to me garish colors. Pink, Purple, Blue...20 rows of chairs, a podium, a picture of a smiling Jesus...

About 40 people could have easily found seating accommodation and in the front about 10 chairs were arranged in a circle. 5 persons, 1 man and 4 ladies had already taken a seat in the circle.

They greeted me warmly and asked me to take a chair. The man appeared to be in charge. He stood up and fiddled with a radio.

Pre-recorded music beamed through a number of speakers hanging high on the wall. Gospel songs.

One more couple arrived and then the organizer got up and changed the tape. It was now a soft music with ethereal overtones. I could not make out what instruments were used, probably electronic."My name is Joe". He said it with an accent, which I realized later was Dutch. "Tonight we are going to meditate and invoke spiritual healing". His hands moved as he spoke, almost as if he was blessing the little circle of people around him. I loosened my tie, it became warm in the room.

"Just take a deep breath in and hold it for the count of 4 and then exhale slowly through your mouth—and relax". I followed his instruction and noticed that the others had straightened themselves in the chairs. Their feet were firmly on the ground and their hands lay on their knees, palms up. I was wondering about the importance of the posture when Joe quietly came over to tell me to take the same position. Uncrossing my legs I sat up straight.

"Take another deep breath through your nose and hold it for the count of 4 and exhale slowly through your mouth—and relax". It became warmer in the room but I did not want to fiddle with my shirt and just prepared to endure.

There was a third breath. Same instructions. He then asks us to close our eyes.

Now I got worried. What was he up to while my eyes were closed. I did not know anyone in the group, matter of fact I had just picked up an advertisement announcing the meditation circle with spiritual healing. The pamphlet bold faced "non-denominational", "Christian" and "guided". While the people around me looked somewhat middle class I had heard too much of various cults who lure people into their clutches with the disguise of meditation or love. I decided to be careful.

Joe looked like a business man. Tall, slender, well dressed, he could have been an accountant. I blamed myself for not finding out ahead of time. Somehow I would have felt more at ease if I had known who the people around me were. It appeared that the others were familiar with the routine.

My decision was firm, I was going to squint from time to time.

The lights in the room dimmed as Joe asked us to relax our body. He must have had a remote control unit. I carefully avoided moving my head too obviously but from time to time I looked at Joe just to make sure that nothing unusual would happen.

Joe instructed us to totally relax all the muscles in our body. His voice was calm and pleasing. The music was turned down and only appeared to be hanging there somewhere in the background.

I heard Joe suggesting to walk through a Garden, watch the flowers, hear the brook.

All of this was to come out of our imagination and somehow I was not getting the pictures of garden and brook. A quick peek at the others in the circle revealed that they were sitting quietly in the seat, eyes closed and somehow peaceful. Joe too had his eyes closed as he spoke. His arms were stretched out like he was embracing the whole group. I tried to concentrate on his voice.

He was invoking a spiritual light to come out of the heavens and suggested that we take the light and use it as a blanket around us. Protection and comfort was supposed to flow from the light. The word comfort reminded me of the temperature in the room. I checked myself and somehow the warmth of the room seemed to have transferred into a comfortable surrounding, neither hot or cold, just comfortable.

The next thing I remember was that Joe was reading a list of names. Did I fall asleep? I felt comfortable and squinted at my watch. According to the time passed, I could have only dozed off for a minute. I decided to be more careful, after all there were only strangers around me.

All the names on the list had some afflictions, which Joe asked the Holy Spirit present to take away. He asked the spirit to heal those people in the name of Christ.

Joe then went on to speak to us to place on our palms all the problems and worries we wanted to have healed. He waited a while and then continued "let the beam of spiritual light dissolve them".

The lady next to me let out a heavy groan. I quickly looked at her and noticed that her body had slumped on the chair, her head on her chest and her arms just dangling next to her.

For a quick moment I wanted to help and get up to wake up the lady, if she was still alive. Her groan could have been her last breath, as far as I was concerned. No one else seemed to be concerned. Joe still had his arms wide open, eyes closed. I did nothing.It was quiet except for the background music. I closed my eyes and tried to concentrate on something that was bothering me to place it into my hands. There wasn't anything I could think of.

The gentlemen across the circle mumbled something. It was not easy to understand but it sounded like "Thank you oh Lord, Thank you."

My eyes once more scanned the room. I still dared only to squint carefully. One of the other ladies had her hands high up in the air, her face pointing to the ceiling. She smiled. Everyone else seemed to be just sitting there, except for the dead lady and Joe, who was standing.

Joe spoke. He told us to gather our soul back into our body and to return to the church.

The music beat became faster, almost as if it was going to wake us up. Joe guided us from the garden back into the chair and suggested that we received a healing from the spiritual beam which apparently was still around us and which we could take with us. The mantle of light was to help us fend off the problems of the coming week.

"Carefully open your eyes to get used to the light", said Joe.

"God Bless you all".

With that he stepped out of the circle and went into a room at the back from where he shouted "there is coffee and tea back here, help yourself".

The group got up and went to the back. I followed and stretched my body. Somehow I felt that I had slept for a couple of hours, but my watch told me, the whole ceremony had taken only about 50 minutes. The temperature in the room felt comfortable. I looked forward to a cup of coffee.

The people in the back room all chatted and laughed and when I entered they looked at me, introduced themselves and told me to feel at home and enjoy some of the home made cookies on the table.

Joe came over and told me, don't worry about your nodding off, it sometimes happen. "Oh, by the way", he said, "you could have placed your little toe on your palm, it would have healed up easily".

I was shocked and almost dropped my coffee.

Joe must have seen the shock in my face because he put his hand on my shoulder and said "It's O.K., you will learn. I put the light around the toe and tomorrow morning it wont hurt anymore." With that I was standing alone with my thoughts.

How did he know that my toe was giving me trouble? I had recently bought a pair of cowboy boots and while breaking them in, my right little toe gave me trouble every morning, until about noon. Then the body seems to have gotten used to it.

Being a healthy person I did not remember the pain I was going through in the mornings when putting on my boots. But now, reminded of it by Joe—how did he know?

I ambled over to the lady who had slumped in the chair and asked her if she was O.K..

"O.K.? I feel great. I had the best healing in a long time. The spirit took me away and showed me my new house. It's red and has a wonderful garden. Just the way I pictured it to be."

I asked a few more questions. No, the lady had not put in an offer anywhere, but she was confident that tomorrow an agent would come by to asked her to view the new home. Yes, she was dreaming of owning a home with a garden, but the money was the problem. Did she know where the new house was going to be? No, just the number she remembered, not the street. 147! "In black wooden numerals", she emphasized with a smile.

Turning to the lady who had smiled and looked upwards during the meditation I asked her what her experience was and she told me of the wonderful message she had received about her uncle being healed of cancer. She still smiled confidently. I admired her trust in the message and did not ask any more questions.

Joe's handshake was firm when we said good bye. "I will see you again soon", he said smiling. "God bless you".

I doubted that I would see Joe again. There were many small groups around town and I wanted to research as many as possible. Not that I wasn't amazed at his message about my toe, but...maybe a lucky guess.

It was about four months later when I received an invitation to a travel industry function. The downtown hotel banquet room was crowded, maybe 1500 people had come to see a presentation by a tour operator.

Suddenly I felt a hand on my shoulder. Turning around I stared at a name tag "Hi, my name is" and then in big black magic marker script "Joe". I looked up. There he was standing tall and smiling. We exchanged business cards. He was a travel agent uptown.

"Good to see you again", he said. I was confused and smiled, lifted my soda glass and cheered "have a nice evening". He nodded and walked away.

After the meditation evening I had often thought of Joe. Particularly the next day. Around noon, I remembered that in the morning my little right toe just slipped into the boot without hurting. Not even noticed at that time, it had come into mind at noon time when someone admired my boots.The little meditation group also came to mind one day when I was driving to a friend's house in the suburbs. His driveway was blocked by a big moving van and I was wondering about him leaving town unannounced. But no, it was not him moving, but he received a new neighbor.

I parked my car a bit up the street and walked to my friend's door when a voice called me to the van. "Hi, this is the house I have been dreaming about. Come by when I have moved in. The coffee pot is always on".

It was the "slumped over lady" who was grinning and carrying parcels from the van into the house. The perspiration from the work made her face look like she had just taken a shower. Her blouse was wet but she was happy. I waved and knocked on my friends door. In big brass numerals he declared that his house number was 145!

# 30

## *Psychics in Flea Markets.*

### *How not to judge a psychic and a very personal psychic message for you!*

It was a nice Summer Sunday afternoon when a friend and I strolled through a Flea Market to see what kind of bargains were available today. Thoughts of books, tools and car accessories went through my mind—but psychic messages?

One of the isles had a draped booth and outside sat a young lady providing administrative backup for a psychic card reader. I was curious. My questions to the lady were fruitless. She was just hired help to make appointments.

"Is the psychic a man or woman?", I ask her.

She just briefly answered "a women".

"How long does it take to get a reading?"

"Ah—maybe a half an hour."

"How much does it cost?"

"$ 35.00."

It sure was not a sales pitch and I had to practically drag further information out of the young women. Looking at her closely, she may have been a High School student—but she sure did not impress me with her ability to sell the services of the psychic. But then—may it was not to be sold, who knows?

I hang around this isle for a while because I wanted to get a glimpse of the psychic. Her name was "Lamarra", something I could not interpret.

Finally the curtain opened and a lady walked out. She was about 40 years old and wore a white T-Shirt with a bird painted on the front and the lettering "I want to be free" on the back. This was not the psychic but the customer. The freedom seeker nodded to the administrator and walked away from the booth.

"How was it", I asked her.

The lady looked at me but she was not looking at me. You know that feeling when someone is in deep thought and their eyes sort of look through you to a far away spot? Well this lady was looking through me all right.

"Fine", she murmured and wanted to keep on walking.

I was curious and needed to get a better answer.

"Did she give you a good reading?"

Now the eyes began to focus on me. There seemed to be some anger showing in her face and sure enough when she spoke she sounded clipped and said "Lamarra got me right here".

With that she was pounding her chest. "She got me were it hurts and I tell you I am going to stop that hurt !"

Her voice was determined now. Tears came into her eyes and while wiping them away with a fist she said "I am going to do it".

With that she walked away. She had a goal. One could see that the way she walked fast through the isle and made a turn to disappear from my sight.

I went back to the booth.

"Can I have an appointment now?"

The student looked at a book and shook her head. I would have to wait for at least an hour to get a reading. With that a gentlemen approached and told the student that he apologized to be late for his appointment. The girl just nodded and pointed to the curtain.

The man was dressed like a stock broker and somehow looked out of place in this environment. But then—you never know.

As the man lifted the drapes to get into the cabin, I peeked and saw the psychic sitting behind a table. A deck of cards in front of her next to an ashtray. I recognized the face. It was one of the ladies from one of the spiritualist churches I had visited. Her white hair was now crowned with something akin to a turban. In the church she was a specialist in psychometrics—reading the vibrations of items that belong to you.

In the church I had not been that impressed with the psychic but the results on the last customer seemed to speak for themselves. Even though, I did not know the details of how the freedom lover got to be so determined.

I decided to forego the wait of one hour.

A few stands down the isle a computer could read your handwriting and gave you a printout on love, money and health. Only one Dollar was required plus your signature. Well I bypassed this one as well.

There was one booth selling "New age tapes". Music to meditate by and messages from channels. One of the tunes playing on the tape machine caught my fancy and I bought it.

Strange to see the psychic movement entering into flea markets. Did this mean that the grass roots were working?

In my music tape I found a colored questionnaire. A free color analysis.

A number of color blocks had to be chosen as "I like best, second best, etc." Mailing the sheet to a company would result in analysis of "Personality, mood and what's happening to you". Well, I could not resist.

Six weeks later a computer printout came through the mail. Reading the analysis I felt good. I smiled to myself. Customer satisfaction should be number one when you sell something and here I got something that made me smile.

I want to share the printout with you. I truly believe that this is meant for you as well, yes you who is reading it right now:

"...you recognize an abundance of opportunities in life and feel the urgency to take advantage of as many as you can.

"You believe in following instructions and completing objectives with an organized plan.

"You involve yourself in personal relationships with caution. You are a rare person...you can be looked up to and recognized as a leader.

"Perhaps you are considering looking for a new position at this time."

Did I hit your personality right on?

That is the trouble with many psychic messages: They are very general. But then, maybe we as people have a lot more in common than we think.

# 31

## *A UFO traveler and my sky watch.*

✦

### *I met someone who has been in the UFO. I am ready to go. My call to Commander Ashtak—*

He was born in one of the Eastern European countries and still speaks our language with an accent. For all intend and purpose he "has made it" in this country.

One day I was introduced to him as the person who had traveled in an UFO. I did a second take.

Here I had been hoping for many years to spot an UFO and there he was traveling in one through the country side.

I remember way back when I went fishing in one of the northern lakes and while sitting in the canoe and hoping for a late feeding bass to strike we noticed this fast moving light in the sky.

"A UFO", I yelled to my buddy.

Pointing to the sky, we both saw the light traveling at what must have been a very good clip. Faster than any plane would go and even higher. It kept a steady course and we followed it until it disappeared in a cloud bank.

The next three nights we saw the same light at the same time and in the same arc. We doubted that it was a UFO and got disappointed.

Some research in the city confirmed, the UFO to us was a well known satellite, plying the skies to document the weather pattern around the world.

This little encounter with the satellite got me to think about UFO's a lot and I read a lot of books and magazine articles about the subject matter.

Some of it I found absolutely unbelievable. Some stories came into the category "could be true."

I even joint an organization which was dedicated to research and investigation of the phenomena. Their newsletter gave me more information and made me a "believer" with the "but I have to see one myself before I 'really' believe" attitude.

Whenever I drove anywhere my eyes were directed to the sky.

It must have been 20 years after my satellite-UFO that I was in the north again and this time the sky was clear and crisp. Snow had recently fallen and the temperature had dipped to minus 30 Celsius. There was no noise except for our feet whenever they touched the snow it made a compacting noise.

We stood still for a while to watch the stars. There was the big dipper, the little dipper, the North Star and Orion.

We talked about how nice it would be to see a UFO and to be really in the know about their size, speed, origin and intention.

There were only two of us and we exchanged thoughts on the many speculations published about visitors from out of space.

Suddenly while looking at the direction of the Pleiades I noticed a moving light. I pointed at it and my partner too saw it. It was blinking.

An aircraft was my first thought but then—it was to high up and too fast to be a jet. There was no noise, just the blinking dot moving through the sky in a straight line.

I could not determine the color of the light, I only saw the blink. My partner later said that it alternated between green and red. These colors give my eyes trouble and I could not confirm the varying colors. But the blink was there.

After following the light with our eyes through a quarter of the sky, the light suddenly disappeared.

There were no clouds, there were lots of other stars, but it just "went off".

Strange as it seemed, we still thought of it as a satellite.

Our real experience with a UFO, if they do exist, will still have to come.

In the meantime, our acquaintance who had been traveling in a space craft and wrote a book about it, is going to conventions all over the world to talk about his experience. He is exchanging information with other Contactees and in general is keeping up-to-date on the UFO scene.

There is only one thing about him that puzzles me: He doesn't really like to talk to "normal people" about his adventures in the sky. He is very shy about it. Matter of fact, one of my friends commented once that he acted kind of "dumb" about the whole thing.

Here are dozens of Humans who are privileged to have been contacted and thousands of others don't keep their eyes off their lips as not to miss a word they are uttering and this fellow is not very talkative to strangers. His book is sold out and there is no reprint planned...somehow it does not make sense to me.

Was he just telling the truth or did he have a motive to invent the story.

If he wanted a publicity stunt, well he had it and could have made money off it—he did not want to. Many of the book royalties went to a small church were he was a lay worker. A New York friend once offered him some money for the film rights—nothing came of it, because he really did not seem to be too eager to get involved.

Strange.

I am sure that one day I am going to make a special effort to investigate the UFO phenomena from a journalistic point of view. I know it has been done but then once I do it myself, I know that the facts are facts. There are no rose colored glasses for me to look through because

I am interested only in the facts. There is no need for me to make up a story to back up my belief. It's that simple—just the facts.

By then I hope one of the aliens has contacted me. A first hand report—the truth.... I am getting myself prepared to beam up. I just hope the aliens read this book to know that I am ready.

# 32

## *A final word.*

### *I traveled, met people, met bums, met psychics. Is the phenomenon real? Are the crooks real? I am ready to find a teacher*

The cases mentioned in this book are only a fraction of the ones investigated. I traveled around the world and every opportunity I got to check in with a psychic, an astrologer, a card reader, tea cup reader or any other "weird" denomination, I took.

Yes, I always approached those people skeptically. Sometimes even with deceit, by claiming, that I had never heard of the phenomena before or never had any experience with it. While this was stretching the truth, I did want them to go all out, unencumbered to convince me as they convinced "Joe" or "Mary" just coming off the street.

I went to places that would not admit journalists, lawyers, police, priests or politicians because they were afraid of debunkers or trouble with the law.

My identity had to be hidden many times. In my search I saw fire walkers—the real ones and the fakes.

The psychic healers in the Philippines, with their chicken blood hidden between their fingers, could not impress me. What did impress me was when I saw one of the healers touch the chest of a child and suddenly this child started to cry.

What was so strange about that? The fact that I had talked to the mother of the child who had traveled from Germany to this island in the southern Philippines in search of help for her deaf and dumb three-year-old.

That was impressive.

Not impressive was the Florida congregation that advertised their "Reverend Jesus" as the incarnation of Christ with the healing power of the Christ.

While I looked a bit out of place in the Hispanic church, I nevertheless could tell that here the almighty dollar was important to the Reverend. His healing examples were stooges, well arranged and well orchestrated to present to the believer a show.

Very little else was demonstrated to the congregation but private services were advertised and appointments could be made right there and then.

On the other hand the lady who ambled up to me at a hotel bar in southern Florida and told me that she saw me while sitting in the lobby and was wondering if I could spare 10 minutes—well, she impressed me.

I was ready to be touched, you know, the sob story about this or that ailment or family problem. Something a few dollars or a few drinks could cure.

My surprise started when I offered the lady a drink and she refused. Matter of fact she said she wanted to get out of the bar and talk to me in the lobby.

When you travel as much as I do, you meet all kinds of strange characters. I happen to like people and even the weird ones will get a chance from me.

They want to talk? I talk. They want money? I sometimes give them money. I like a good sales pitch. I listen intently to what they have to say. Questions will get me more information.

Some of the bums I have met are good. They have honed their pitch to sound believable. Some even show you papers and news clippings to back up their stories. Some are simply pitiful. Depending on the mood I am in, I give them something for their work. After all, that is their job. They earn their money that way. I would not want that job—and you probably neither.

Let me quickly stray to an occurrence in Washington. I was walking through the old Georgetown area. A man stopped me and asked for change. I questioned him about the purpose for the money. He said he wanted to eat something.

This is were I put in the first check: Is the guy really hungry or does he want to buy drugs or booze? I offered to buy him a hamburger. He looks up very surprised and says "OK".

We walked into the nearest hamburger joint, one of those franchise operations. The manager comes from behind the counter and assails my bum with something like 'I told you before not to set foot into this establishment, blah, blah, blah'.

The manager even went as far as turning the man around by his shoulders to move toward the entrance cum exit. The bum did not say a word.

I intervened and talked to the manager "excuse me, sir" !

It was tough to get his attention. He was determined to throw out the unwanted customer first, before dealing with me.

"This man is my guest! Leave him alone!", I shouted at the manager who looked stunned, first at me, then at the bum.

There was a short silence, then some mumbling, which could have been a curse, then an apologetic gesture towards me and an explanation.

"We cant have those guys in here, they just bother our customers", the manager talked to me but looked at the bum.

I must admit that my guest did look somewhat shabby with his coat 3 sizes too big, his dirty pants and "holy" shoes. But I was determined. I ask my dinner partner if he was going to bother any of the customers in here and he said "no".

That was good enough for me and we walked toward one of those plastic tables to sit down.

It must have looked funny to some of the patrons, as I introduced myself formally to the Hobo. He mumbled, "My name is Jack".

"O.K. Jack, what do you want to have to eat?".

He settled on a Hamburger with French Fries and a Coffee.

Here was a bum who was hungry, you could see it.

Between some bites and sips he told me the story of his life.

Just once he stopped, looked me square in the eye and said "Your business here in Washington will take a strange twist tomorrow. First your deal will not be signed. Secondly one of your appointments will be cancelled and then you will meet with your third appointment and they will make you an offer which will make you glad that the day went the way it went.

He went on with his life story and ignored all my questions about the message he had just given me. He just shook his head.

After the meal I gave him a few dollars. He thanked me, looked at me strange again and mumbled, "I want to check in to the men's hostel. You need to bum a buck to get in, you know".

With that he rushed away but not without looking at the manager and waving a "thank you" at him as well.

The lawyer I met the next morning told me apologetically that his client had to withdraw the offer. My second appointment was cancelled. When I met with my third group I got an order that I could not have handled if I had signed number one and number two.

I thought of the bum and sent him a thank you though the air. Hopefully he would get it. It's a strange world we live in.

Back to Florida. The lady sat down and quickly came to the point. I guessed her age to be in the 70's and from the outside appearance she could have been anybody's grandmother. Well dressed, well spoken.

She said "young man, you must listen very carefully, because I can say this only once....".

I was all ears. Her story had religious overtones. The world was coming to an end and I was selected to survive that disaster. I would find some friends who would help me to be prepared when the time came.

It was not the atomic war I was to worry about, but pollution. Our environment was to collapse and many people would die. Our governments would be falling and chaos would be on the streets. I was to pay close attention to my inner feelings because I was one of the survivors.The information came like a machine gun from the lady. She hardly stopped to take a breath.

How did she know all this?

"Joshua is in touch with me".

She showed me quickly a couple of books she had written and published and told me that she would send me some information on the upcoming end of the world.

With that she packed her little bag, in which she carried her books and made me solemnly swear that I would listen to her and watch out for the impending upheaval. She whizzed out of the place before I could come out of my daze.

Just another religious nut.

That was my quick judgment and with that I went back to the bar to finish my beer.

I had forgotten about this lady until one day a parcel arrived at my house. It was a "home made parcel" with second hand wrapping paper. My name was not quite spelled right and even the address had mistakes in it, but obviously the postman must have thought it belonged to me.

It did.I almost fell to the floor when I opened the package. On top was the book that I had seen in the ladies cotton bag. Two more little books were enclosed as well. All of them talking about "Joshua's messages".Religious fervor can take on a determinism second to none. I know, because I have been approached to be saved by dozens of different organizations. Many of them persistent. They are at my door step every weekend.

Here I had not been expecting the same drive, the same vision. But I was mistaken—obviously.

Why am I so perplexed about this situation? Simply because of the following facts:

I did not give the lady my name or address!

Easy, you might think, she got it from the hotel. Well, hold on. The hotel bar I was sitting in was 35 miles away from the hotel I was staying in. I was in this hotel only because they had advertised in the local paper to have entertainment and my hotel was not having any.

It so happen, that I had made a mistake in reading the advertisement. The entertainment was only on weekends. This was the middle of the week. Therefore I thought 'one beer and back to the TV in my room'—when the lady interrupted me.There was no one in this hotel who knew me, no one who would know were I was staying for the night. And if you know southern Florida, you also know that within a 35 mile strip there must be at least 500 hotels—and I think I am conservative.

This is a puzzle to me. I often thought I should investigate and check with the publisher to trace the lady, but something is holding me back. Something inside of me says 'leave her alone'.

I haven't even read all of her books. There seems to be still time for me to get to that. The same something inside is telling me this.

Yes, this lady was good at whatever she was doing.

Not so good was the gentleman who offered "free readings" if the information given was not 100 % accurate. Well, this seemed to be a sure bet. Particularly since the fellow had his leaflets in all the hotels. They must have had good reports about him—would they distribute his flyers otherwise?

It was in Southern California and my appointment was made by phoning a number and leaving the name and the room number of the hotel on an answering machine. Later a message came back with the time of the appointment and the address of the place.

I went. It was a motel room. A burly African-American fellow opened the door. "Are you the Psychic?", I asked.

"No, I am just the doorman", was the answer.

The psychic was white skinned and his hair had left him with the exception of a tiny curl in the middle of his head. He looked funny. I thought anybody who looks like this must be good to stay in business.

The reading started by him asking me a lot of questions. Where I came from, what I was doing, why was I in Southern California?

I stopped the flow of questions by pointing out, that I was to get a psychic reading, that he was to supply information to me and not the other way around.

The psychic mumbled. He then took out a black velvet cloth that was embroidered with all kinds of symbols associated with mystic philosophy. There were stars, the crescent of the moon, a pyramid, the sun, astrological signs, Egyptian symbols...all in all it looked like a hodgepodge to me and I was wondering what all the symbols had in common to be of value to the psychic. I soon found out.

He told me that the reading was to be $ 50.00. I had to put the bill on one of the symbols of my choice. I did. The sun was my favorite.

He then rolled up the cloth and placed another cloth over it, or so I thought. I realized afterwards, that I should have kept a better eye on my money, a well worn $ 50.00 bill.

The doorman was taking a chair next to me and listened to our conversation.

I could not believe my ears when the psychic started to talk to me and gave me the same information that I had just given to him in response to his questions.

I waited silently.

No more information from the psychic. He had closed his eyes and just sat there.

I asked him whether I should ask questions about anything for him to answer, because I found the silence silly.

He opened his eyes and said, "well, that is all".

He now rolled up the cloth again and then I noticed the paper underneath, but my $ 50.00 were gone. He must have done some quick fingering to rearrange the cloth and put the money somewhere else.

My protest fell on deaf ears. The psychic did not utter one more word. His sidekick did however.

"Did the man not give you accurate information ", he asked with a strong southern east coast accent.

"Well, he told me what I told him", I said.

"No, man, this is information coming from the universe", he argued.

It went back and forth a number of times and then the doorman stood up and towering over me he wanted to know if I was accusing the "good man" of anything irregular.

The "good man" was just sitting there. His eyes closed he looked funny, even now, when I realized that I was just about to be taken for 50 bucks.

And so it was.

Yes, I could have reported it to the police. I did not. I only had one more day in town, and I was not about to come back for a trial or what have you, if one would take place at all.

These con artists move in to town and out of town very quickly. Usually the bell men in the local hotels get a few bucks to put out the flyers. When trouble comes, nobody wants to get involved.

I did not either. Even though I threatened to call the police and inform all the hotels.

In reality I just phoned the local tourist information centre about the clown who was going to ruin the reputation of the town.

I don't know whether anything was done.

I never saw those folders again in my travels.

Entertainment is part of this whole scene. There are groups who invite a psychic for a birthday party and in tea rooms patrons can get their tea leaves read by some more or less "professionals". Some of these people do it full time and make a living off it. Some do it for fun and extra spending money.

Some are good, as I said, some are bad.

There is one thing that came out of all the investigations. I became even more curious. I wanted to find out what the forces behind the true psychics were. That some of those people that I encountered had some extraordinary powers was quite clear to me. On the other hand, no one was able to demonstrate with a click of their fingers some divine power to manifest gold or diamonds. But then maybe the true psychics are not into jewels, golden jewels that is.

I decided to find a teacher. A demonstration by another person was not good enough for me. I needed to know what I could do—only then would I be convinced.

0-595-25022-X

Printed in the United States
32908LVS00005B/313-336

9 780595 250226